REFINED

by

FIRE

Mary Potter Kenyon

REFINED
by
FIRE

A Journey of
Grief and Grace

MARY POTTER KENYON

Endorsements

"When we experience grief, what we long for most is the hand of someone who knows the depth of our pain. *Refined by Fire* is a friend's hand as you travel your journey of loss. It is the gentle, compassionate voice of someone who's walked in your shoes and who knows the rocks beneath your feet. Mary Kenyon brings practical experience clothed in gentle grace, unflinching truth, and unwavering hope. I recommend this book to pastors, therapists, and anyone who has lost a loved one."

—**Shelly Beach**, Award-winning author of 10 books, including *Precious Lord, Take My Hand*; Managing editor of *Hope in the Mourning Bible*; Co-founder of PTSDPerspectives.org, Caring.com expert, and ShellyBeachOnline.org/PTSDPerspectives.com

"Mary Kenyon's *Refined by Fire* reminds me of my grandmother, Madeleine L'Engle, who taught so many of us that writing can be a form of prayer that leads us to grace. I was moved to read how her influence inspired Mary to write and heal as well. Mary's writing style is extremely accessible, and her voice raw, authentic and brave. By the end I was crying with her. I would definitely recommend her book to anyone who is going through any type of loss."

—**Léna Roy**, granddaughter of Madeleine L'Engle, author of *Edges*, and seasoned writing instructor and Program Manager for Writopia Lab, a not-for-profit dedicated to empowering youth through creative writing.

"Not long into the writers' workshop I was teaching on a Midwestern college campus, a woman in the front row of desks began to weep. I didn't know why at the time. But I sensed I was witness to something holy happening in that room. The book you hold in your hands is a result of that holy moment when the God of heaven gave the author permission to write out of the midst of her pain to provide a holding-on place for others in theirs. Mary Potter Kenyon's breathtakingly real thoughts reveal that razor edge where despair dances with hope and the ugly becomes elegant. I'm already creating a list of those laid on my heart to receive the gift of the story of Mary's grief journey."

—**Cynthia Ruchti**, author of Ragged Hope: Surviving the Fallout of Other People's Choices

Contents

Published by Familius LLC, www.familius.com

Familius books are available at special discounts for bulk purchases for sales promotions,
family or corporate use. Special editions, including personalized covers, excerpts of existing
books, or books with corporate logos, can be created in large quantities for special needs.
For more information, contact Premium Sales at 559-876-2170
or email specialmarkets@familius.com

Library of Congress Catalog-in-Publication Data
2014941871

pISBN 978-1-939629-34-0
eISBN 978-1-939629-53-1

Printed in the United States of America

Edited by Maggie Wickes
Cover Design by David Miles
Book design by Maggie Wickes

10 9 8 7 6 5 4 3 2 1

First Edition

Acknowledgments

For every book written there are those people who have inspired, encouraged, and stood by the author. This book was written during a particularly difficult time—in the two years following my husband's death. First and foremost, my eternal gratitude to David, the husband who, despite his death, remains the wind beneath my writing wings and whose wise advice still echoes in my head: *Slow down. Relax. Don't worry so much. Tell the truth.*

Thank you to my sisters who dropped everything to rush to my side that terrible morning, the cotton batting that surrounded me with love and tender care in the days following David's death.

David was so proud of his eight children. This book couldn't have been written without the encouragement of each of them. For Dan, my oldest son, never regret having gotten so close to your dad during his cancer. He was so very proud of you. He worried about you being alone, and I truly believe he had a hand in leading you to someone to love.

For Elizabeth, my oldest daughter: You were never able to properly mourn your father because you were immersed in caring for Jacob. I cannot imagine the magnitude of your own grief. I am in awe of your grace and example of faith.

For the son-of-my-heart, Ben, I will always count you among my children. I am so grateful that David had you as a friend. I cannot tell you how many times he came home laughing because of something you said or did at work. He loved you, but even more important—he liked you.

To my son, Michael, I will never forget, and neither should you, how you overcame your natural aversion to hospitals to visit your dad after his heart attack. I am grateful that through the loss of him, you and I learned to hug again. I look forward to those hugs.

And to my dear daughter Rachel, whose tender heart suffered so with the loss of a father who shared interests in things your mother doesn't care about: plants and animals. I appreciate all the meals you heated up for me in those early days and the hugs we share now.

For my Matthew, on the cusp of adulthood when your father died, you moved out within a few months of his death, and I was secretly glad when you returned for a few months a year later. I wasn't quite ready to see the "man of the house" leave.

And to my three youngest girls, Emily, Katie, and Abby, we formed a special bond, a sort of "team" at home after your dad's death. Not a day went by when one of us didn't lament, "I miss Dad." I am so very sorry for the terrible loss you three have experienced at such a young age and so very grateful that you made allowances for a mother who miserably failed at so many things, but whose love for you remained constant, and always will. Make your daddy proud, girls.

For my friend, Mary Jedlicka Humston, who took me out to lunch every month for more than a year and who dared to ask the questions no one else dared ask: *How do you stand it? Does it always hurt, or does it hurt less sometimes, and more other times?*

For dear friends, my "sister" Lois and "brother" Ron Hixon, David was glad to call you brother and sister when you visited the hospital daily after his heart attack. Thank you for being there for both of us.

Thank you to the Cedar Falls Christian Writers Workshop family, and especially authors and mentors Shelly Beach and Wanda Sanchez. For the many strong women I met through other writing conferences I attended, including Judith Robl and Cynthia Ruchti. For the women sitting at a breakfast table in Wheaton, Illinois, who upon finding out it was my wedding anniversary, prayed out loud for me. "How beautiful they are," I was surprised by the level of love I felt for virtual strangers, even as I realized that is how God wants us all to live.

For Cecil "Cec" Murphey, whose books meant so much to David first, and then to me, and whose generous scholarship made it possible for me to attend the Write-to-Publish conference in 2012, where the seeds of this book were planted. There was an instant connection when we met in person that fall. I am honored to call you friend.

For Timothy Juhl, my "poet and wanderer of the Universe," and fellow survivor of loss.

Thank you to my Bible study family, who walked a path of self-discovery with me, sharing a hunger for understanding God's plan for our lives.

To Lydia, the young woman who listened to the nudges of the Holy Spirit, sending me pages of Bible verses when I'd prayed for them. Your support for our family in these past few years has been tremendous. I've loved you like a daughter for a long time, and as I write this, you will soon become one.

To my publisher, Christopher Robbins and the entire Familius family, I extend gratitude. I feel extremely blessed to be a part of a company with such strong values, and I love watching you grow.

Thank you to my editor, Maggie Wickes, and her patience with what must have seemed an author's eccentricities at times. I appreciate the long hours you put into editing this manuscript.

And, finally, to Beth Gerken, my first "widow" friend who became my strongest prayer warrior, and to the widows and widowers I hope to help with my words.

There are countless others to thank in this endeavor: many more family members and friends, along with seemingly random strangers who touched my life through my grandson Jacob. My world is so much bigger now. Whether or not we have connected on Facebook, know that our lives are forever linked through the short life of a beautiful child, and something much bigger than ourselves. May the "Force" be with you.

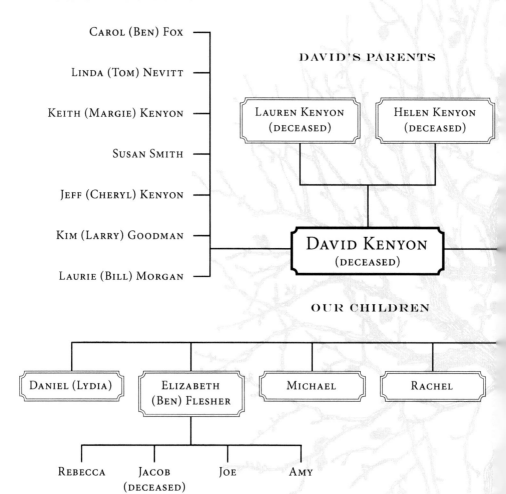

DAVID'S SIBLINGS

Carol (Ben) Fox

Linda (Tom) Nevitt

Keith (Margie) Kenyon

Susan Smith

Jeff (Cheryl) Kenyon

Kim (Larry) Goodman

Laurie (Bill) Morgan

DAVID'S PARENTS

Lauren Kenyon (deceased)

Helen Kenyon (deceased)

David Kenyon (deceased)

OUR CHILDREN

Daniel (Lydia)

Elizabeth (Ben) Flesher

Michael

Rachel

Rebecca

Jacob (deceased)

Joe

Amy

Roots of "Support"

The Bible

Cedar Falls Writer's Workshop Participants and Shelly Beach and Wanda Sanchez

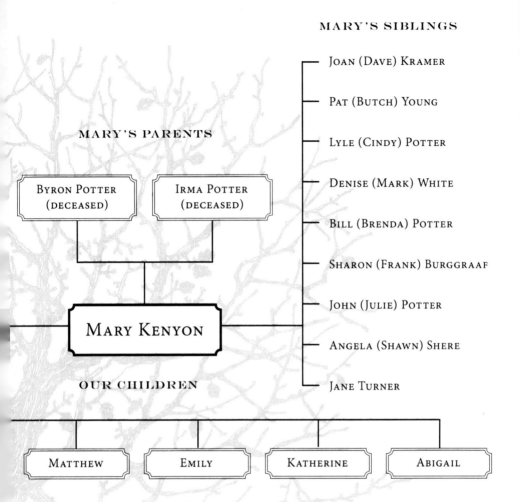

MARY'S SIBLINGS

JOAN (DAVE) KRAMER

PAT (BUTCH) YOUNG

LYLE (CINDY) POTTER

DENISE (MARK) WHITE

BILL (BRENDA) POTTER

SHARON (FRANK) BURGGRAAF

JOHN (JULIE) POTTER

ANGELA (SHAWN) SHERE

JANE TURNER

MARY'S PARENTS

BYRON POTTER (DECEASED)

IRMA POTTER (DECEASED)

MARY KENYON

OUR CHILDREN

MATTHEW

EMILY

KATHERINE

ABIGAIL

FAMILY TREE *of*
SUPPORT

MARY'S FRIEND, MARY JEDLICKA HUMSTON

MARY'S BIBLE STUDY "FAMILY"

WORDS FROM AUTHORS WHO HAD GONE DOWN THIS ROAD BEFORE MARY: MADELEINE L'ENGLE, C.S. LEWIS, AND H. NORMAN WRIGHT; AND CECIL MURPHEY, WHO TRAVELED IT AFTER HER

Foreword

by Cecil Murphey

I started to write, "I enjoyed this book," and then I paused and asked myself if it was all right to say that. But the truth is, I did enjoy it. Yes, it's sad in places, and Mary Kenyon has that special ability to write with deep emotions that spill over the entire page. Many times I wiped away tears and thought, I understand—I've felt like that too.

Even though her coping with grief was different from mine, there was also a warm sameness. She lost her husband of thirty-four years; I lost my wife of fifty-eight years. Mary's loss happened more than a year before mine. We met in person about seven months after David's death, and again, about seven months before the death of my wife.

In *Refined by Fire*, Mary candidly shares her pain, her uncertainties, and especially her dark moments. She doesn't give up. As she discovers hope, she passes that on to her readers.

In her final chapter, she quotes her friend, Judith Robl, who wrote, "The holes in your heart never fill in, they simply quit bleeding so profusely." Although those were Judith's words, they sum up the heart of this beautifully written book.

After my wife died, I received a total of 15 books through the mail (and the best ones came from Mary). I had written books on grief, been a pastor for fourteen years, buried both parents, outlived three brothers and the same number of brothers-in-law, two nephews, and a number of people who were very close to me, all of which left me with deep sadness. In some ways, I was a professional on grief and loss. But I was also a man whose heart was broken by the loss of the most important person in his life. I hurt just like any other grieving spouse.

Shortly after Shirley's death, I read brief portions of Mary Kenyon's still-in-progress book, *Refined by Fire*. The sincerity and compassion of her prose touched me. She says in true heart language what so many of others could only point to or felt but were unable to explain.

For instance, in an early chapter she copies her blog entry and twice states, "Tell the truth." She wondered if the words would scare others, but she wrote them anyway. At times her grief was so acute she didn't know if she could go on; she cried in the parking lot of a grocery store; her pillow was often wet with tears. But she didn't hide her pain from readers. Living with the grief enabled her to keep going and also offer encouragement and comfort to those who are yet behind her.

Yes, she wrote painful, heart-wrenching statements, but that's how grief affects many of us. Several times I've said to my friends, "Grief sneaks up and attacks me at the most inappropriate times." But I was determined not to hold back and to cry if I needed it—and Mary exemplifies that same determination.

Two items in particular have stayed with me and caused me to do a lot of thinking and remembering. One was the question about taking off her wedding ring. Like everyone who has lost a spouse, I also had to make that decision. Shortly after Shirley's death, I put her matching ring on the little finger of my right hand and it was comforting to feel both rings on my hands.

Shirley died in the spring, and by early fall I still had not decided when—although I knew I would eventually take off both rings. On the last Sunday in October, I sat by myself in church and unconsciously played with my wedding ring. At one place in the sermon, the pastor spoke about moving on and letting go of the past. I listened and heard the words but didn't absorb what he said.

Just then, and to my surprise, I twisted the ring and it came off. As I stared at it, the pastor said, "God never calls us to stop. It's always a forward move." I grasped the message God was giving me through the pastor's words.

Second, Mary writes, "I'm not sure when I realized I was studying grief, instead of just experiencing it. After reading dozens of books that dealt with someone else's grief, it occurred to me that if God had given us a world in which there would be so much loss, he would surely have designed us to withstand it."

She goes on to say that her friends moved on with their lives and she was left behind. But she also learned that God had given her the ability to face the loss, even though tears flowed.

To some those words may have little meaning, but I realized that God created us to withstand the vicissitudes of life. Especially for those of us who are believers in a compassionate God, we also know that spiritual resources are there for us to live with and to grow from.

I've long advocated re-using our pain. That is, we experience what seems like insurmountable problems, and yet, we eventually overcome them. Because we have been in the deep valley of isolation and darkness, we can quote the words of the apostle Paul who writes of our merciful Father, who "comforts us in all our troubles so that we can comfort others. When they are troubled, we will be able to give them the same comfort God has given us" (2 Corinthians 1:4, NLT).

Another way to say that is only those who have experienced deep loss can write about it meaningfully so that the message brings healing to the brokenhearted.

Thank you, Mary Kenyon, for sharing God's healing power by touching me with your words in my grief.

Grief at Ten and a Half Weeks

Journal entry, June 8, 2012

It's dawning on me that I will never be loved like David loved me, no matter how much my children, my siblings, or my friends love me. I will never again feel that special love or hold his hand or hug him or kiss him. I still leave the kitchen light on every night and I'm not sure why, but he was the one who always turned it on, and I just can't bear to turn it off. Yesterday I bolted out of the grocery store when I began crying in the peanut butter aisle because David loved peanut butter sandwiches. I've yet to make it through a Hy-Vee without crying because I spot the deli where he sat and drank coffee and read the newspaper while I shopped. We never experienced an empty nest, never traveled outside of Iowa together, or flew on an airplane, or went to a concert. I cry every Sunday during Mass because I used to hold his hand in church, and now I see older couples holding hands and realize we will never grow old together, and I miss him. I miss him, I miss him!

Everything makes me think of him. I hit the buttons on the ATM machine and remember how hard I laughed when he kept touching the screen instead of the buttons. He looked over at me and I was laughing so hard I couldn't speak so he started laughing too. There we were, sitting in a car at the ATM, laughing so hard we cried. Then we went out for a shared banana split and laughed some more. And I don't think I will ever want to eat a banana split again.

Everyone says "Thank God you have the children," and I think yes, but it is because I have young children at home that I cannot scream, cannot even moan in the night with an eight-year-old next to me. This morning I watched Abby singing at Vacation Bible School and I looked for some joy, some laughter, or even a tidbit of happiness from her. Mostly, it is anger. She called me stupid after the program because I couldn't find the shirt she'd made, so I sobbed in the car and then I really felt stupid. Stupid, stupid! Stupid with grief!

"I hate you!" she railed, and I saw the horrified looks on the faces of the other women, saying loud and clear that I am a horrible mother with an awful child. On the way home I took Abby to the gravesite and we both sobbed, hugging each other, and she said she was sorry and she doesn't know why she says those things.

I can't stop writing and talking about it, even to strangers. A support group e-mail I get in my inbox every day informs me that at some point people might get bored with grief and it would no longer be appropriate to share with them. Am I at that point? Because maybe it is now, at ten and a half weeks, that I'm supposed to be "better." And how will I know who I can continue to share my grief with? I want someone to tell me what to do. Tell me what to do, please tell me how to do this!

Scene of Domestic Bliss

Grow old along with me! The best is yet to be.

–Robert Browning

The kitchen was quiet except for the soft sound of my pen moving across paper and the intermittent rustling of book pages being turned on the other side of the table. Intent on completing the rough draft of my weekly newspaper column, I barely noticed when David rose to refill my coffee cup. Soon, I'd transfer everything to the computer and print it out for him to look over. In the past year my husband had become more than just supportive of my writing; he was now my first reader, critiquing my choice of words and spotting errors.

I sensed David's gaze. Glancing up, I smiled and thanked him for the coffee, then returned to my writing. When I looked up again a few minutes later, his eyes were still on me, with a look I'd begun seeing more frequently of late—that of complete and utter adoration.

"What? What are you thinking about?" Married for nearly thirty-three years and the man could still make me blush with his transparency. The children were asleep, but I knew one of them could walk downstairs at any moment. If he was contemplating what I thought he might be, his timing was off.

"I'm thinking how beautiful you are, and how talented. You sit there and all these words just flow out of you."

My face warmed. I hadn't washed my hair, applied makeup, or changed from my ratty pajamas, and my husband still thought I was beautiful? I knew he must be seeing through the eyes of love—seeing the nineteen-year-old girl he'd married.

We had an enviable marriage by early March of 2012, an easy companionship centered on love, commitment, and putting each other first. We'd finally figured out the *agape* sort of love described in the Bible—selfless and giving. Our relationship hadn't always been that way, which was why it was all the more incredible in its richness. David's bout with cancer in 2006, and my stint in caring for him, had triggered the difference.

This is what God meant marriage to be, I reflected that morning, realizing not for the first time how lucky I was to share my life with my best friend.

"I wish everyone could have what we have," David echoed my thoughts.

"I love you. You're a beautiful man." His baffled look and the slight shake of his head amused me. He'd never understood why I'd begun describing him as beautiful during his cancer treatment, but the description was apt—David was beautiful, inside and out.

And three weeks after that kitchen table exchange, he was dead.

Faith of Our Mothers

I gave my life, but until it was finished, no one can know what that life gave. My death is not mine. It is yours. It will mean what you make of it. Whether my life and death was for good or for nothing, it is you who must say this. I leave you my death. Give it meaning. Remember me.
(Source unknown, written in the back of one of my mother's notebooks)

My mother was diagnosed with terminal lung cancer in the summer of 2010, just four years after David's cancer. She lived less than three months after her diagnosis, dying in November, on my birthday. The night of her death I experienced what could be described as a shift in faith.

For most of my adult life I'd remained that little girl who had lain completely still in her bed after her mother left each night, worrying over the words in a simple child's prayer: "If I should die before I wake, I pray the Lord my soul to take."

Why might I die before I wake up? Can children die? What could happen to me while I sleep? If I could die, should I even go to sleep? Will my parents die in their sleep? What was dying like? My thoughts ran wild, and my limbs trembled in that dark bedroom of my childhood.

That same little girl who'd so feared dying grew up to be an anxious adult. I refused to teach my own children the prayer that included that ominous phrase. The fear of death never quite left me, surfacing under duress. Watching my grandfather die in a hospital when I was eighteen and unexpectedly, and prematurely, losing my father in 1986 had not

3

dissipated my fears. But on the night my mother passed away, my long-held fear of dying ceased. Perhaps it was the way she'd faced death or her anticipation to be with my father. Maybe it was watching my siblings gently care for her as she lay peacefully dying. After a lifetime struggle to impart her faith to her children, through her death, my mother had somehow managed to leave me a legacy of faith.

My mother had been a consummate artist and a highly creative woman. Having lived in poverty for most of her life, she didn't have much in the way of material things. When it came time for my siblings and me to divide up her possessions, it was her art we coveted—the paintings, wood carvings, and handmade teddy bears. As the writer in the family, I became the "keeper of her words," inheriting many of her notebooks and several unpublished manuscripts. I also had a thick memory book she'd filled out for me. During the months following her death, I read and reread her writing. With my husband's blessing, I also spent many hours alone in her empty house that winter, working on a book. David encouraged my lone writing sessions, hugging me goodbye at the door and handing me a travel mug of hot tea he'd made me for the road.

During breaks from the intensity of writing, I'd push my chair back from my mother's vintage oak table and stand up to stretch, walking through the house and poking through the remaining boxes. I immersed myself in her creative spirit, paging through homemade scrapbooks she'd fashioned from brown paper bags sewn together. At home, I would repeatedly leaf through her memory book and notebooks, reading about her two greatest desires for her children: to live a life utilizing their God-given talents and to ultimately get to heaven.

I netted more than just quiet writing time from those cold winter days I spent in my mother's house, writing and looking through her things. I got a glimpse into her soul, and though I didn't realize it then, into my own future as well.

The Muse, the Mother, and Kenny G

Blog post on March 12, 2011

Yesterday I sat at my mother's table, waiting for the muse to strike. I put on a kettle of water to boil, lit the cinnamon candle on the table, popped a Kenny G CD in my laptop, and opened the door to the other room so sunlight would stream through the house. These are the rituals that I have incorporated into my mini-writing retreats at my mother's house.

My fingers hovered over the keyboard for a few moments, but my mind seemed devoid of ideas, my brain blocked. Alarmed, my gaze darted around the room, searching for some inspiration, something to jumpstart my creativity.

I left the table and wandered through the rooms, images of my mother flitting through my memory. She sat on this chair, used this end table for her coffee. She watched television here, leaning her elbows on her knees, smoking a cigarette. She worked on her paintings out here on the porch. I paused near a box of books and bent down to look through them half-heartedly. I'd already gone through them several times already. I realized with a start that I had already looked in every box, fingered every scarf, rifled through every scrapbook and notebook, and inspected each delicate dish in the cupboard. Treasures come in the form of tiny pieces of paper inside things and notations in my mother's neat handwriting. "My father, William Weis, made this." "Bowl of my mother's, Elizabeth Weis."

I'm not sure what I continue to search for. If I am looking for something, it isn't in my mother's empty house. There are no hidden messages or more treasures to find.

That stark realization hit hard and I felt the undercurrent of sadness pull me in. Tears streaming down my cheeks, I was soon gulping back noisy sobs and wiping at a runny nose. I laughed wryly, imagining how I would look to a stranger peeking in the window. The image helped compose me.

The sadness we carry within ourselves, the gaping hole in our heart, is not ours alone, though it feels that way at times. The loss of a loved one is a universal truth we all face at some point in our lives. Books have been written about this journey called grief. We can read a dozen of them and imagine how it will be for us. I thought to lose my father was bad enough; to lose my mother was one hundred times worse. I imagine to lose my husband would feel like searing the flesh off my bones.

I imagine to lose my husband would feel like searing the flesh off my bones, I'd written just twelve months before I would discover the truth of that statement.

Making Sense of It All

That was one of the worst things about losing your wife, I found: your wife is the very person you want to discuss it all with.
—Anne Tyler's *The Beginner's Goodbye*

"You don't need to write this down," the funeral director commented when he saw me frantically taking notes during our meeting the day after David's death. "We'll handle everything."

"But this is what I do. I write," I responded, acutely aware of how many times I'd said the same to David. My two oldest children on either side of me nodded.

"Where is the 'Handbook for Widows'?" I'd asked the director earlier as he'd walked us through displays of guest books and memorial cards. It was surreal, to think of myself as a widow. Weren't widows old ladies? And yet, as I sat at that table frantically scribbling on a legal pad, I remembered that my mother had not been much older than I was when she'd planned my dad's funeral. That gave me strength. She survived— maybe I would, too.

"How do I do this? When will it stop hurting so much?" I asked out loud in those early days of grief as my sisters circled protectively around me. They just shook their heads in response, their eyes filled with compassionate tears. They had no answers for me since they hadn't been down this particular road of grief. I am sure that my own eyes must have reflected what I was feeling: shock, desolation, and despair. I began to wonder if my sisters had actually made up a "Mary chart" to stagger their visits so that it was never more than twenty-four hours between visits, no more than twelve between phone calls. I pictured Denise looking at her watch in the middle of the afternoon, calling out to her husband, Mark, in the other room, "It's my turn. I have to go see Mary," and I could even imagine his loud answering sigh. Angela would have come home from work, changed her clothes, and started supper before glancing at the clock and gasping out loud. "I haven't called Mary today. I have to call her!" Jane phoned regularly and Pat stopped to see me after work. I was able to smile as I thought about these strong, loving women—sisters who were also my friends.

"How are you doing?" When my sisters asked me that question, I'd go silent as I assessed how I was feeling at that exact moment. Most days, the best answer would have been that I was *functioning*. I'd rise at 6:00 a.m. and make my way down the stairs to put on coffee, studiously avoiding the sight of the small kitchen light above the coffeemaker. David had always been the one to turn it on, and I couldn't bear to turn it off. In those first three weeks I did the bare minimum each day, allowing my visiting sisters to wash dishes while I sat at the table, numb, glancing from the clock in the kitchen that had stopped ticking the day of David's death to the one on the office wall, which was equally useless, as it had also stopped working. It would be mid-April before anyone changed the batteries, just one more thing that David had always been responsible for. If it weren't for the leftover roast beef and mashed potatoes from the funeral luncheon, I'm not sure I would have eaten during those early days of grieving. My daughter Rachel would visit every day after work, heat up a plate of the comfort food, and place it in front of me as I waited for nightfall and an appropriate time to collapse into the bed I'd once shared with my husband—a bed where I was now joined by an eight-year-old with a broken heart.

It did not escape me that for the first time in months, I had nothing scheduled for three weeks, nothing pressing to do after the planning of the wake and funeral. I spent most of each morning on the couch or in the kitchen, listening to a Christian music station and writing in my journal, trying desperately to make some sense of it all. How could David be there one day and gone the next? I knew my mother had conducted a similar ritual of writing after my father's death because I had her notebook pages to prove it.

On the morning after my husband's wake, I filled three pages in a journal with sentences and sentence fragments:

> The opening of doors for my writing and workshops just since my mother's death, preparing a way for me to make an income.
>
> Emily's involvement with a youth group just this past year. Her recent urge to hug David several times a day.
>
> Our family had just recently begun listening to a Christian radio station.
>
> David had started reading Joyce Meyer books and watching her program on television.
>
> David kept telling me he was proud of me, that I was soaring; it was my time to fly. He'd been gazing at me for longer periods of time, telling me how beautiful I was. It was happening so often, I'd actually been getting embarrassed.
>
> David's life insurance policy being reinstated so recently, just twenty-seven days before his death.
>
> David wanting the *Getting to Heaven* book at the hospital, co-written by Cecil Murphey and Don Piper, when he hadn't wanted any other reading material I'd tried to leave with him, not even his favorite magazine. *90 Minutes in Heaven*, by the same authors, had been his favorite book.
>
> An envelope arriving in the mail on the day of David's death, with a check for fifty dollars for an essay that will be featured in a Cecil Murphey book.
>
> Receiving an e-mail the evening of David's wake, informing me I'd won a Cecil Murphey scholarship for a writer's conference that would end on what would have been our thirty-third anniversary.

I'd always relished the idea that those who went on before us might be able to reach out to us in some way from beyond, or that there might be something more than mere coincidence in the events of our lives. As I jotted down these random circumstances in my journal, I saw a clear pattern emerge. I gradually realized that the events of the past months seemed less random and more as if God had been preparing our family for the loss of David in very tangible ways, from my increasingly profitable workshops and public speaking engagements and the reinstatement of a life insurance policy all the way down to the radio station we'd begun listening to shortly before David's death.

Those songs brought me a great deal of comfort. The first time I realized just how comforting music could be was the morning of David's funeral when I started my vehicle and Matt Redman's "You Never Let Go" began playing. *Oh, no you never let go. Through the calm and through the storm.* I pulled a notepad out of my purse and wrote those words down so I could look them up later. *Oh no, You never let go, In every high and every low. . . .*

I had never felt lower in my life. Nor had I ever felt closer to God.

Finding My Way

When I married I opened myself to the possibility of great joy and great pain and I have known both. Hugh's death is like an amputation. But would I be willing to protect myself by having rejected marriage? By having rejected love? No. I wouldn't have missed a minute of it, not any of it.

—Madeleine L'Engle, in *Two-Part Invention: The Story of a Marriage*

"Mary, are you ever sorry?" The woman stopped me on the lawn outside of the building where we were attending a Christian writer's conference. I'd seen her wiping away tears at the lunch table earlier as I described what my marriage had become—how for five and a half years after his cancer treatment, my husband and I had experienced what it was to be truly loved.

"Sorry for what?"

"Sorry you got that close to your husband only to lose him and hurt so much?" Tears streamed down her cheeks again, and I knew what she was going to say next even before she said it. "Because I'm not happy with my marriage, but I'm almost scared to try and fix it, in case I lose him."

"No! I'm never sorry for that." My reply was more vehement than I meant it to be, so I softened my voice. "I consider the last five years of our marriage to be bonus years. I might have lost him to cancer and never have known what marriage could be."

"My husband doesn't even know there is anything wrong."

"David didn't either." I smiled at the memory. "He never knew how unhappy I'd become. He just thought that was the way marriage was

11

supposed to be. But once our relationship changed, he was so grateful for that kind of love." I paused. "I'd never rubbed his feet before."

A look of confusion crossed her face.

"For twenty-seven years I'd never touched his feet. Then one afternoon, after a long day of chemotherapy and radiation, he was so tired he collapsed in the chair. I knelt before him, removed his socks and shoes, and began gently rubbing his feet. He was startled at first, but then relaxed. What if that was all it would have taken to make my marriage better years before? Me rubbing his feet and putting his needs first? We truly cherished one another. I experienced *that* kind of love. Some people never do." She nodded her head in understanding.

Time had slowed those first days after David's death, and not just because of the broken clocks in my house. As the initial numbness of shock wore off, it hit hard—my husband was gone. How could I go on alone? It was incongruous to me that I was going through such a huge emotional upheaval without David to share it with. He'd been at my side for every pivotal event in my adult life.

Having experienced such a beautiful marriage relationship, how could I bear the loss of it? In those first hours and days after his death, surrounded by my adult children and sisters, I wasn't sure I *could*. I had no precedent for this kind of anguish. It felt as though someone had ripped open my chest, leaving a gaping, bloody wound.

I had not been raised to memorize Bible verses, nor as a child had I heard the adults around me praying anything other than rote church prayers. Yet, it was Bible verses and spontaneous prayer I yearned for those first days after David's death. It was not that I was raised in a faithless home. On the contrary, my parents had been devout Catholics. But studying the Bible and verbalizing our faith in spirit-led prayer had never been a part of our religious upbringing. That explained the behavior of some of my siblings when, after David's death, I tearfully asked them to pray with me.

"Of course," was their heartfelt response, and then they took my hands, bowed their heads, and remained like that for a few moments as I waited expectantly. While they were fervently and silently praying for me, I unexpectedly found I needed to hear the words.

I hesitantly divulged this to my fifteen-year-old daughter, Emily. She urged me to visit her youth group leader, who was good at "praying out loud." So two weeks after my husband's death, I rode my bike to the Methodist church three blocks away and knocked on the door of the twenty-five-year-old youth leader's office. Teary-eyed, I explained why I'd come. She pulled me into her office, shut the door, took my hands in hers, and prayed out loud for me and my family. Peace and comfort washed over me.

Despite not ever having learned to study the Bible, there were verses that were familiar to me from reading and hearing them repeatedly. The first Bible verse that came from the deep recesses of my mind after David's death was one regarding "giving thanks in all things." While it was a stretch to thank God for anything the morning of his death, I was intensely grateful for the love that David and I had shared. I began writing out prayers of thanksgiving in a journal two days later. Years before, I'd had a hardcover journal personalized with a photo of David and me on the front, but not sure how I'd use it, I'd stashed it in my supply cupboard. I pulled it out after David's death and began writing. The handwriting was pretty rough. My fingers thick with grief, it took extreme effort just to lift the pen and write across the page.

> Thank you for the time I had with David. Thank you especially for the last few years with him as my true partner in the sense you meant a marriage to be. Thank you for the support of the new Christian friends you brought me just in the last year. Thank you for my children.

Writing had always come easily for me. I'd written my way through many tough times, including David's cancer in 2006 and the death of my mother in 2010, but this felt different. Writing David's obituary was heart-rending. Working on anything else seemed impossible at first, and yet I couldn't help but write. Somehow, writing about him kept the memory of David alive. I was journaling every morning—disjointed sentences, observations of grief, and of course, the continued prayers of thanksgiving. The words felt stilted, full of raw pain, yet they answered the questions of whether I was sorry for having loved David so much.

> Dear Lord, thank you for letting me have David for as long as I did. Thank you, especially, for what I think of as our "bonus years," the five and a half years since his cancer. Those five years were the best years of our marriage and we truly cherished each other in a way that I wish that everyone could have. I have known true love. Thank you for taking David in a gentle way. Thank you, too, for the eight children left behind, the adult children who are a tremendous comfort to me, and the younger ones who keep me focused on a future.

On May 5, just a few weeks after David's death, my friend Mary visited from Iowa City, intent on getting me out of the house. She treated me to lunch, and we spent the day together. That evening I was able to write these words of hope in my journal:

> In the darkness of grief, I set out on the journey of the rest of my life; one foot in front of the other, my hands splayed out in front of me, feeling for the light. And then comes a fleeting moment when a laugh escapes me during lunch with a friend, and I get a glimpse into the brightness ahead, and think in surprise, *Oh, someday I might be okay.*

I would wonder why the prayers of my childhood had not sufficed when my husband died. It was those rote prayers I had turned to less than two years before when my mother passed away. I would discuss this with my friend Mary and my sister Angela in an attempt to figure it out. Eventually, I did. I wrote the answer in my journal on the morning of December 24, nearly nine months after David's death:

> Angela visited last night and we talked about prayer. I told her the rote prayers of childhood were not what I needed after David died. They helped after Mom's death. Why wasn't that enough after my husband's death? I pondered that again this morning—what was the difference? When Mom died, the wound was deep, and it hurt. But when David died, it went right through the bone, to my very core—leaving a huge gaping hole. I needed more than the prayers of my childhood to bind up such a wound.
> I needed God's Word.

First Holiday

Blog post on April 9, 2012

Easter has never been a huge celebration in our house, so I thought it might be an easy holiday to endure without David. Still, I'd already discovered I couldn't face the candy aisle or even the prospect of moving the pile of stuff in front of the attic door to unearth our Easter baskets. I was grateful my sister Angela offered to let my children decorate Easter eggs at her house Saturday afternoon. We always decorated Easter eggs, and it didn't seem fair to take yet another thing away from eight-year-old Abby, just because of *my* grieving. The fact that I hadn't even managed to boil the eighteen eggs I brought with me didn't seem to faze Angela. While she put the eggs in a pot to cook, I sat down to watch the hustle and bustle of the familiar activity and even managed to decorate a few eggs myself. It was when Abby showed me the egg she'd made for her daddy that I felt the room shift. I suddenly couldn't breathe. David hadn't participated much in the preparations for Easter, but there were two things I could count on: Abby would always make her daddy a special egg, and David would help me hide the eggs outside on Easter morning, if the weather permitted. Now I was alone, and Abby had no daddy.

I asked Angela if I could leave Abby at her house for a while. The sobs started even before I got to the van. I drove directly to the cemetery. Blind with tears, I tumbled out the door and ran to the gravesite where I plopped down onto the wet grass. I didn't sit there long, only long enough to cry out, "*Why did you leave me alone? How am I going to do this without you? I love you so much.*" In the next instant, I was glad for Abby's youth and resilience. She hadn't expressed any sorrow while she made the egg.

I thought back to her extreme reaction to a small transgression just two days before. Her wailing had gone way beyond the normal range, even for her. When she stomped up the stairs and slammed the bedroom door, I held my tongue. She was a fatherless child, it had been less than two weeks since she lost her daddy, and I needed to be patient. Inside her room, she'd bitten her pillowcase in anger and frustration, and then heard a small renting of the material. As she explained it later, she hadn't meant to continue as she knew it was wrong. She'd bitten and ripped the pillowcase, first with her teeth, and then with her hands, until it lay in shreds around her pillow. When I saw it that evening, I eyed the torn material dispassionately, intimately understanding what she must have felt.

On Easter morning Emily, Katie, and I got up at 5:00 a.m. to attend a Sunrise Service in a park, leaving Matt and Abby home asleep. When we got home Abby was waiting on the couch, looking dejected. "Did you see your Easter things?" I asked, and she shook her head no. "We aren't doing Easter, are we? There aren't any eggs hidden outside."

I pointed to a few small toys, sidewalk chalk, and candy on the floor beside the couch. I hadn't even bothered with an Easter basket. No wonder Abby hadn't thought we were celebrating. Compared to the carefully orchestrated Easter baskets I usually prepared, this pile looked desolate and pitiful.

I stuck a ham in the oven and worked on my weekly coupon column before heading to church and yet another service. Dan, Michael, Rachel, Elizabeth, Ben, and their respective children joined us for our Easter meal. By late afternoon, with most of my children off having fun at the park and just two of my grandchildren and Abby at home, I was feeling weepy again. Jacob was hungry and nothing sounded good to him except a Burger King hamburger, so I made a quick decision. Knowing how little appetite a person can have when they are going through che-motherapy, I wasn't about to miss out on providing the one food Jacob craved. I grabbed the "Dad" egg out of the refrigerator and loaded the kids in the van. When I turned right instead of left at the stoplight on Franklin Street, Becca piped up that I was going the wrong way.

"Yes, I know. I want to give Grandpa his Easter egg."

My two grandchildren and youngest child didn't seem to think there was anything odd in my behavior: stopping at the cemetery to deliver a single colored egg to a gravesite on Easter day.

Later that night, before she fell asleep, Abby expressed a slight disappointment in our dismal holiday, but quickly added, "Maybe next year will be better."

Yes, maybe next year will be better.

Word Study

You never know how much you really believe anything until its truth or falsehood becomes a matter of life and death to you. It is easy to say you believe a rope to be strong and sound as long as you are merely using it to cord a box. But suppose you had to hang by that rope over a precipice. Wouldn't you then first discover how much you really trusted it. . . . Only a real risk tests the reality of a belief.

—C. S. Lewis, *A Grief Observed*

When my husband was diagnosed with cancer in 2006, my prayer life pretty much consisted of "Help" and "Please," and God answered both with supportive friends, family, and a husband who survived. My mother, who was diagnosed with lung cancer in August of 2010, was not so lucky. She died two and half months after her diagnosis. My five-year-old grandson, Jacob, was diagnosed with cancer a month after that and went through some pretty rough treatment before being declared cancer free in 2011. Then in March of 2012, Jacob's cancer returned.

I will never forget that moment when I informed David that the little boy he loved so dearly was going to have to endure further cancer treatment. We stood on the porch together. His arms folded around me as I sobbed into his chest.

David spent the rest of that afternoon raking our backyard. His shoulder hurt that night, but it often did with strenuous exercise since his cancer treatment. Over the next few days his pain increased, and he experienced extreme fatigue, along with a general feeling of malaise. Within a week, his shoulder pain had definitely moved to a discomfort in his chest, and I took him to the emergency room where we were informed that David had experienced either a large heart attack or a series of smaller heart attacks. He had surgery and spent the next nine days in the hospital. I brought him home on a Friday. On the following Monday morning, our doctor pronounced him healing well.

On the way home from that appointment, David quietly asked, "Why would God allow cancer in a little boy?"

I just shook my head in response. It was a question I'd asked myself many times.

"If I could go, and he could stay, I'd go in an instant," my husband continued. I knew the truth of that statement. David would have given his life for any one of his children or grandchildren. He would have given his life for me.

That next morning I found my husband non-responsive in his recliner. Sometime during the night his heart had stopped, and I thought mine had broken in two. In my extreme emotional distress, I wasn't sure where to turn. Family and friends surrounded me with their love, but I still floundered. I needed something more.

Like my parents before me, I owned a Bible. I owned several, in fact— nice, hardcover leather-bound volumes. I would pull one from the shelf every Christmas Eve, brush off the thick layer of dust, and read out loud the story of the birth of baby Jesus, stumbling over all the *thee*'s and *thou*'s. I'd always found the Bible difficult to read, but after David's death I needed the comfort that could only be found within its pages. But I didn't have a clue how to even begin to find answers in a Bible. When I told my fifteen-year-old daughter this, she gave me a soft-cover study NIV Bible that a friend had given her. I flipped through the pages and found the language much more user friendly. I wondered how I could have reached the age of fifty before holding a study Bible. I prayed for guidance in using it, even reaching out to a self-avowed born-again Christian I knew. I never heard back from that person. Instead, within days of my prayer an envelope arrived in my mailbox. The same young woman who'd given my daughter the NIV Bible sent me two pages of

Bible verses she'd written on plain notebook paper.

"Something prompted me to write these down for you," she wrote. "I hope they help you in some way."

I was particularly drawn to these two:

> God heals the brokenhearted and binds up their wounds. —Psalm 147:3

> A father to the fatherless, a defender of widows, is God in his holy dwelling. —Psalm 68:5

A week later, I was contracted to do several devotions for a grief Bible. I'd never written a devotion, but I welcomed the challenge. I knew that in order to accept the assignment, I would have to immerse myself in the Bible, learn to look up verses, and apply them to real-life situations. I began by picking up some devotional books and studying their formatting, copying down pertinent verses that touched my heart. I then imagined ways my own grief stories might help someone else.

Besides the Bible, I was gravitating toward the grief section at every bookstore and library I visited. I surfed Amazon listings for more titles. Somehow it helped to read about the grief experience of others. When I'd asked the funeral director where the "Handbook for Widows" was, I'd been serious. I really did want a handbook that would walk me through the rough terrain of widowhood and tell me exactly how long the pain would last and when it would wane. I found strength from the words written by those who had gone down the road of grief before me. Their words illuminated that what I was experiencing was not all that unusual and might even be considered "normal." I started with Madeleine L'Engle's *Two-Part Invention: The Story of a Marriage.*

I'd had L'Engle's *Two-Part Invention* on my bookshelf for years, shortly after I discovered her Crosswicks Journals series. I'd devoured *A Circle of Quiet* first, identifying with it so much that I was eager to read the others. Despite the differences in our lives, L'Engle and I shared the particular challenge of combining motherhood and writing. We also both delighted in the companionship of our husbands. It had been very painful for me to read this particular book in the series—a chronicle of her marriage and her husband's subsequent death. My body shook with sobs the first time I read *Two-Part Invention* shortly after my own husband's cancer experience. How could L'Engle bear to watch her beloved in pain? I'd seen David's desperate pain after his cancer surgery and hoped I'd never have to see that again.

I could only imagine the particular anguish of spousal loss then, but imagining is a way to prepare oneself for the inevitable. As I read it a second time, after David's death, I copied down passages like this one:

> But grief still has to be worked through. It is like walking through water. Sometimes there are little waves lapping about my feet. Sometimes there is an enormous breaker that knocks me down. Sometimes there is a sudden and fierce squall. But I know that many waters cannot quench love, neither can the floods drown it. (page 229)

After Madeleine L'Engle's *Two-Part Invention*, I read *A Grief Observed* by C. S. Lewis, then Joan Didion's *The Year of Magical Thinking*. I was heartened by the fact that I actually did shave my legs when C. S. Lewis saw no point in shaving his face without a spouse there to touch it. I was strengthened by the fact that I quickly disposed of David's shoes while Didion kept a pair or two "in case he came back." L'Engle's spirituality encouraged me in my search for a sustaining faith. H. Norman Wright's *Reflections of a Grieving Spouse* was especially helpful, so much so that I ordered extra copies to share with others. Despite his own training as a grief and trauma counselor, Mr. Wright was not prepared for the sudden emptiness when his wife of forty-eight years passed away. Through short chapters that included entries from his own journal, he walked readers through the journey to healing and a new chapter in life. I completed it in short bursts over a period of two days, thankful to have read that my repeated mention of my widowhood was one of the listed natural reactions. "Why do you insist on telling everyone?" one of my daughters had asked, wondering why I continually spoke of my loss at every opportunity, even with strangers in the aisle of the Target store. I didn't know why and wondered if it was not quite sane to do so.

According to Wright's book, it was a perfectly normal response. For me. Each person has their own way of grieving. Some symptoms of "normal" grief Wright listed:

- Distorted thinking patterns
- "Crazy" or irrational thoughts
- Fearful thoughts
- Feelings of despair and hopelessness
- Out of control or numbed emotions
- Memory lags and mental short circuits
- Inability to concentrate
- Losing track of time
- Shattered beliefs about life, the world, and God
- *Want to talk a lot* or not at all (emphasis mine)

He reiterated that each of these responses was completely normal and contended that grief takes longer than we would think, intensifying at three months, on special dates, and at the one-year anniversary of the partner's death.

I wasn't just reading books about grief. Hungering for a connection to David, I began reading his personal books from our bookshelf. While books had always been a huge part of our life together (we home-schooled and had once owned a used bookstore), David had not always been a reader. The fact that he had not only begun reading avidly in the year before his death, but had specifically requested certain authors and subjects intrigued me. I wanted to discover what it was that had drawn him to books like Cecil Murphey's *90 Minutes in Heaven* (written with Don Piper), Todd Burpo's *Heaven is for Real*, and anything and everything written by Joyce Meyer. Besides reading her books, in those last few months he'd also spent an inordinate amount of time flipping through television channels, searching for Joyce Meyer broadcasts. After his heart attack, I'd brought half a dozen of his favorite magazines and books to the hospital to entertain him. He'd shaken his head wearily, saying he couldn't concentrate on reading. I took all the books and magazines back home with me. Then one day, as I sat in a chair near his hospital bed, he asked what I was reading. His eyes lit up when I replied that it was the newest Murphey/Piper collaboration. He told me to leave it with him. *Getting to Heaven* was the last book David touched. I would never know if he'd actually read it, but the knowledge that he had held it in his hands gave me a sense of comfort as I finished it later.

It occurred to me as I read the books he'd chosen in those last few months: David must have been going through a faith journey of his own.

Reading Grief

Trust one who has gone through it.

—Virgil

"It gets worse at three months," one author wrote.

"Five months," someone at a grief support group maintained.

"A year. It was much worse the second year," another in the group stated firmly, and I saw several heads nod. The pain would be worse the second year? I'd been looking for emotional sustenance through these grief support meetings, not discouragement.

Initially, I latched onto the Bible and spiritual books written by Christians to help me through grief. Those books served as a sort of life vest—a bungee cord to God. Greedy for grieving words, soon I was reading anything even remotely pertaining to grief, including novels. I immersed myself in grief reading, through the spring and into the summer, taking notes in my journal when something resonated with me. I laughed through Lolly Winston's fictional *Good Grief* with the widow who wore her pajamas to work. How many times since David's death had the simple act of getting dressed overwhelmed me? There had been several days early on when I hadn't even bothered.

Some books disappointed me, especially those that offended my moral sensibilities. Did I really need to know that the author of *Making Piece: A Memoir of Love, Loss and Pie* had a two-night stand with a stranger she met in a bar a few months after her estranged husband's death, or that some of the women in *Saturday Night Widows* "just wanted to have fun" in a way that would also extend to sleeping with new boyfriends?

But it was Joyce Carol Oates with her *A Widow's Story* that affected me far more than any other non-spiritual book I would read.

"Why, exactly, is it that you are reading a book like that now?" my son Daniel chided one day when I informed him the book was making me cry. Why indeed? Not only had my crying increased, but the lyrical prose of the author's vivid description of her distress was actually pulling me down into a sandpit of darkness I'd already climbed out of. For the three days I was reading it, I was mired in her sadness, which magnified my own sorrow.

Oates's magnificent writing detailed her grief so vividly that she managed to pull me into her downward spiral. Initially, that was cathartic for me. *Someone else went through this. Someone else understands.* I identified with the particular horror of not having been at my spouse's side when he died, and not being able to say goodbye. (*How could I not have immediately known my beloved was gone? How could I have sat near him and not sense that? How could my husband's heart just stop beating when he'd seemed to be doing so well after his heart attack? Did I even kiss him good night the evening before?*) These were my thoughts that paralleled those of the author, whose husband seemed to be recovering well from pneumonia when she left him one evening at the hospital, only to have him take a turn for the worse and die before she could get back.

It was after 350 pages of despair, despondency, and agonizing pain that I began to wonder about the depth of the author's sadness in regards to the period of time she had been grieving. Surely it had been months, perhaps even a year. No, I realized when I looked at the dates again. It took 350 pages for Joyce Carol Oates to detail less than *two months* of the pain and the sorrow over her loss. Just two months! I quickly flipped to the last few pages. Surely in 416 pages, Oates would at least reach the end of the first year of grieving. It appeared so at first, with these poignant and powerful words on the last page;

> Of the widow's countless death-duties there is really just one that matters: on the first anniversary of her husband's death the widow should think *I kept myself alive.* (emphasis added)

Then I turned back a couple of pages and noted the date of the last section of the book: August 2008. Her husband had died in February of 2008. Oates managed to write 416 pages chronicling just the first six months of widowhood—six agonizing months that included many references to her squirreling away pills in case she needed them to commit suicide. I set her book aside for a moment and turned to the Internet. What happened to this woman, this author who had suffered so greatly after her husband's death? She'd been so thin, so fragile looking. Had she also died of a broken heart? Because of recent research I'd been conducting, I knew that according to some sources, the chances of the surviving spouse dying increases by as much as 60 percent in those first six months of grieving. I fully expected to discover that Joyce Carol Oates had died within a year of her husband.

On Wikipedia, I unearthed this nugget of information:

> In early 2009 Oates married Professor Charles Gross, of the Psychology Department and Neuroscience Institute at Princeton. After six months of near suicidal grieving for Raymond Smith, Oates met Gross at a dinner party at her home.

I felt as though I'd been slapped. Joyce Carol Oates took her readers through the darkest recesses of her mind and into the most intimate corners of her grief. She let us wallow in her misery. She pulled us into a whirlpool of grief with her. As a grieving widow who had not yet reached that magic one-year anniversary, I felt cheated. It would have helped me to know that Oates had found happiness again. I checked the copyright date of the book: 2011. Perhaps the manuscript had been completed before Oates met Gross, before she herself understood that her life was not over. Couldn't she have added a postscript instead of declaring that a widow's greatest accomplishment in the first year was that she "kept herself alive?"*

I abandoned the book for the better part of a day, pondering. *What was it about this book that I found so disconcerting? What was the major difference between Oates's book and Madeleine L'Engle's? What was missing from her book that I found in abundance in the writings of*

L'Engle, H. Norman Wright, and C. S. Lewis? I flipped through the book, observing that outside of a Saint Terese statue on her dresser, Oates made no reference to God, prayer, or heaven. Surely by book's end, she could have included encouragement to the reader beyond the cessation of her evening sleeping pills? She seemed just as spiritually bereft as she was emotionally. It hit me then: what was missing from more than four hundred pages of mourning was HOPE! There was no hope in her chronicle of grief, and without hope, there was nothing for either the author or her reader to hang onto.

> *Future editions of the book did indeed include mention of Oates's remarriage.

A Study in Grief

Grief is a tidal wave that overtakes you, smashes down upon you with unimaginable force, sweeps you up on its darkness, where you tumble and crash against unidentifiable surfaces, only to be thrown out on an unknown beach, bruised, reshaped. . . . Grief will make a new person out of you, if it doesn't kill you in the making.

—Stephanie Ericsson

I'm not sure when I realized I was actually studying grief, instead of just experiencing it. After reading dozens of books that dealt with someone else's grief, it occurred to me that if God had given us a world in which there would be so much loss, he would surely have designed us to withstand it.

After the initial "surrounding of the guard" (my friends and sisters), everyone else seemed to move on with their lives, while I was left behind, to either wallow or rally. Despite my children's continued grieving of their father, I was grieving a partner, the other half of myself. I felt abandoned in the land of the living. I knew only one widow, an old college friend who had reconnected with me on Facebook while her husband lay dying. The timing was uncanny. Her husband died from lung cancer just a few months before my mother did, and her mother would die not long after my husband's death. Beth was my age, and the only widow I knew personally, yet we rarely saw each other in person. Instead, she had become a leader of my Facebook prayer warrior team.

I couldn't even look to my mother for support. I lamented the fact that I'd never really discussed her widowhood experience with her. How selfish I had been when my father had died. If she'd needed to talk to someone about her emotional distress, I hadn't been available to listen. I did remember her having mentioned she'd walked out to the pasture after my father died to cry out in anguish, practicing the old Indian art of "keening." "I screamed and wailed, and it helped," she'd said.

I hadn't understood then. I did after the loss of David.

Remembering those words of my mother's, I googled phrases like "Indian rituals in grief," "mourning garb," and "keening" on my computer. I found this from the Encyclopedia of Death and Dying (deathreference.com) under Native American religion:

> Among many tribes, mourners, especially widows, cut their hair. Some Native Americans discarded personal ornaments or blacked their faces to honor the dead. Others gashed their arms and legs to express their grief. California tribes engaged in wailing, staged long funeral ceremonies, and held an anniversary mourning ritual after one or two years. Southwest Hopi wailed on the day of the death, and cried a year later.

Considering how I felt those first weeks, these seemed perfectly understandable responses to loss. I'd cut my hair very short the morning of my mother's wake, mimicking her own style when she knew she would lose her hair during cancer treatment. Unless I shaved my head, it really couldn't be cut any shorter for my husband.

I could imagine the satisfaction that might come through gashing an arm. The pain of profound loss was already there. . . . Perhaps a self-inflicted wound could theoretically take the mind off the gaping wound of loss? But wailing in a pasture made much more sense to me. I went so far as to ask my son Michael if I could "wail in his woods," as he was the one who had purchased my mother's acreage. Remembering his grandmother's comments, he'd agreed, but I hadn't actually taken him up on the offer. I still wonder if doing so would have helped my healing.

I also read about "widow's weeds" and wondered if it would help or hinder my grief if I draped myself in black crepe and a dark bonnet for a year like the Victorian widows. While the idea that everyone would immediately identify me as a widow was appealing, I shuddered to imagine the state of my mind if I hadn't been allowed to mingle with society during the first year. Nor was I enchanted by the ritual of making jewelry from a beloved's hair after death. When someone had asked me if I wanted to cut locks of hair from David's head before the casket was closed, the suggestion struck me as a bit creepy.

I found that I was studying grief as though it was a college course, and the only way I'd pass was to fully understand it. Along with chronicles of grief, I read books like *The Other Side of Sadness: What the New Science of Bereavement Tells Us About Life After Loss* by George A. Bonanno and *The Truth About Grief: The Myth of Its Five Stages and the New Science of Loss* by Ruth Davis Konigsberg.

I filled pages of my journal with passages like this one:

> Sadness helps us make these kinds of adjustments by giving us a forced "time-out." Sadness slows us down and, by doing so, seems to slow the world down. Sometimes bereaved people even say that living with the sadness of loss is like living in slow motion. There seems to be less need to pay attention to the world around us, so we are able to put aside normal, everyday concerns and turn our attention inward. (*The Other Side of Sadness*, page 32)

This had certainly been true for me. In the months following David's death, I coveted solitude. For the first time in my life, I could shrug off minor annoyances, even the loss of the second agent I had acquired for representation of the book I was working on. The worst had happened: I'd lost my beloved spouse, so little seemed important after that.

In *The Truth About Grief,* Konigsberg delved into the difference between resilient grievers and chronic grievers, maintaining that people are more resilient than the proliferation of grief counseling and support groups would have us believe. Just as I'd concluded, Konigsberg maintained that since loss is so much a part of life, we are built to withstand it. These books had me rethinking my search for the perfect support group I had assumed I'd needed. I'd tried several: an online widow and widowers group and two others that were conducted in my area. I abandoned the online group when I realized that the most active on the message boards had either been very recently widowed, or had been widowed years ago and were still not functioning well. I considered the two grief support group meetings I'd also attended, recalling my horror when the women on either side of me sobbed uncontrollably over the deaths of their husbands not months, but *years* before. I didn't want to be the widow eight years out from her loss, still unable to function, nor did I want to be pulled down into the pit of despair along with widows who were struggling with their own grief. *The Other Side of Sadness* categorized this type of grief as "prolonged," but maintained that it was the exception, not the rule. In other words, those in the early stages of grief could assume that not only would they survive their loss, but they could eventually even thrive in a new life without their spouse.

I became fascinated with the difference in grievers, with statistics of spousal death after loss, and with studying the science behind it. It turned out there was a great deal of medical research behind the theory that someone could actually die of a broken heart.

In the January/February 2013 issue of *Psychology Today* magazine, I read about a study that was reported in *Brain, Behavior, and Immunity*. Lead author Mary Frances O'Connor, a psychologist at the University of Arizona, found that acute stress adds to inflammation in the body, increasing the likelihood of succumbing to heart attack, stroke, or illness. Besides susceptibility to bereavement stress, the altered living arrangements of the surviving spouse could also contribute to the increased rate of death.

What about those widows who have the most difficulty adjusting to life "without," as H. Norman Wright phrased it in *Reflections of a Grieving Spouse*? Was I doing better than some other widows because I had developed a life outside of David through my writing and workshops? That was what my widow friend Beth had intimated.

"Don't look to me for support," she'd warned when I reached out to her through an e-mail after a particularly bad day.

"I'm not doing very well," she continued. "I couldn't stop traveling that first year. I took the kids all over the United States. When I finally stopped running away a year later, I crashed. I had to deal with my grief. I didn't know who I was without my husband."

Thanks to the encouragement of a supportive spouse, I did know who I was. David had been very proud of my writing and the workshops I'd been conducting. He'd been so supportive, in fact, that I'd begun calling him the "wind beneath my wings." I reflected on these points as I continued to read about, and study, grief. I thought back to the inspirational writing of C. S. Lewis and Madeleine L'Engle. Then I contemplated once more the profound despair of Joyce Carol Oates, a prolific author who'd had a writing career outside of the realm of her husband. There had to be more to it than that. Once my friend Beth faced her loss head-on and dealt with it through therapy sessions with a Christian counselor, I saw a marked change in her. She joined a Bible study, started doing things on her own. "I'm happy," she gushed the next time I saw her, three years out from her loss. She could finally see a future for herself "without" her spouse.

It wasn't just a life outside of a spouse that made the difference, I decided. Beth had found something to hang onto: a hope for a future. The difference was *hope*. I needed hope.

Glimmers of Hope

You will lose someone you can't live without, and your heart will be badly broken, and the bad news is that you never completely get over the loss of your beloved. But this is also the good news. They live forever in your broken heart that doesn't seal back up. And you come through. It's like having a broken leg that never heals perfectly—that still hurts when the weather gets cold, but you learn to dance with the limp.

—Anne Lamott

One day as I was carrying a basket of laundry down the basement stairs it occurred to me that I hadn't cried about David for more than twenty-four hours—not even a sob in the darkness of night. I stopped still on the landing and the basket slid from my hands, splaying dirty laundry all over the steps. I immediately sat down and began crying about not crying because I never wanted to forget him. In the next instant, I wiped away my tears, realizing that I would never forget David, but that didn't mean I had to cry every single day.

Eight weeks had passed since the morning I'd discovered my husband dead in his recliner. While my sisters were no longer visiting daily, I would not soon forget their tender ministrations during those early days when I'd felt the need to repeat my sordid tale over and over: How I'd come downstairs and saw David in the chair. How I'd thought he'd just fallen asleep in front of the television. How I went into the kitchen to make coffee, filled a glass of water, sat down on the couch nearby and began writing a letter to my friend Mary, and still did not know David was dead. My sisters knew I needed to repeat that horrific fact to anyone who would listen; that I'd been sitting so near his body and did not know my beloved was dead. I observed the look of shock and pain in their eyes that mirrored my own, noted the subtle glances between them that signaled they might be concerned about my mental health. They had every reason to be.

One aspect of grieving I'd only considered briefly, after my mother's death, was the effect that sorrow could have on the brain. I was losing things—losing my mind, it felt like. Where was the certified document that proved I'd purchased a gravesite? The newspaper clipping my friend Mary had sent about a grief camp for children? Why couldn't I remember the date of my daughter Emily's surgical consult to have her wisdom teeth removed? In a desperate attempt to stem the very real possibility of overdue bills and charges, I began paying bills immediately upon their arrival in the mailbox. Never before had I been so efficient in my bill paying, realizing when subsequent bills arrived that I had actually paid one of them twice.

I wondered how soon a grieving spouse would be expected to return to a full-time job, and how they managed it in the fog of grief. I was grateful I didn't have full-time work. Just my weekly column and the occasional workshops. My first two newspaper columns practically wrote themselves because the Sunday before David had died, he himself had given me ideas for the next two week's topics. My first couponing workshop wasn't scheduled until mid-April, nearly three weeks after David's death. Even then, I wasn't sure I could stand in front of a room full of strangers and talk about something I no longer cared about. David had been my shopping buddy. How could I talk about an activity that reminded me so much of him? The two-hour power point presentation consisted entirely of slides from our shared shopping trips. For a month before my first couponing workshop in November 2011, David and I had conducted strategic shopping sprees in order to obtain the pictures that would demonstrate couponing strategies.

I'd even asked my doctor for advice. "Do you think I will be able to do my April workshop?"

He'd shaken his head sadly and answered truthfully, "I don't know."

Each time I considered cancelling, I remembered David's obvious pride in my writing and the couponing and writing workshops I'd already done at community colleges and libraries. I'd had a busy stint of workshops the week David was in the hospital after his heart attack, including two workshops on the Saturday after he came home. I hated leaving him alone with children that Saturday, but I had two couponing workshops scheduled for Saturday and another one that Monday evening. David insisted he'd be fine, and I should keep my commitments.

Whenever my mind went to the morning I found him dead in the chair, I consciously replaced the image of his slack-jawed expression with one of his face that Monday evening when I came home from the workshop. I'd practically glided through the front door, I was so happy. David, relaxed in his chair, straightened when he saw me, his broad smile lighting up the room.

"Did it go well? It looks like it did," he'd commented as I'd walked over to the chair and leaned down to give him a big hug. David had reveled in seeing me utilizing my talents and enjoying my work. Whenever I'd worry that he was feeling left out of all my activities, he assured me that he loved watching me. "He was so proud of you," family and friends informed me after his death, which of course made it all the more bittersweet and lonely to continue those activities without him at my side.

I got a taste of what it might have been like for David to watch me soar one night when I called my son-in-law Ben to ask if Abby was done playing. His boisterously cheerful reply was so unlike him, I was taken aback. It struck me then that I hadn't heard true happiness in his voice since David's death. Not only was Ben the father of a seriously ill child, he'd lost his best friend when David died. I was thrilled to hear something akin to joy in my dear son-of-my-heart's voice. When I walked down the block to their house to pick up Abby, Ben met me at the door, opening it wide so I could see the results of a day's work replacing the old carpet with new wood laminate flooring.

"It's a surprise. I hope she likes it," he said referring to my daughter

Elizabeth, who would soon be returning from the hospital with Jacob after a week of cancer treatment. My heart leapt at his obvious joy. I realized then what David might have experienced when he observed my happiness and enjoyment in pursuing my passions, and what my sisters and friends were likely looking for in me again. If they truly loved me, they would want to see a return of some of the joy I'd exhibited before the loss.

I'm not sure I would have been able to face that first April workshop after David's death without my sister Joan's support. Not only did she agree to go along with me to the women's "morning out" event where the workshop was being presented, but she encouraged me to stay over-night at their house the night before, saving me a good fifty minutes of driving time that morning. I was happy to take her up on the offer, no longer confident in the internal alarm I'd counted on for more than thirty years. David and I had abandoned the use of an alarm clock many years before due to the infants and toddlers that shared our bedroom. I wasn't sure how it worked, but I'd discovered that if I informed my brain what hour I had to wake up, I'd automatically wake up within minutes of that precise time, without fail. While David had initially doubted my dubious "gift" of an internal alarm clock, he eventually trusted it, even the time we had to leave the house at 3:00 a.m. for his July 2006 cancer surgery. Since David's death, however, I hadn't had to wake up at a specific time and I was so emotionally spent, I wasn't sure I could trust my internal alarm any longer, and I certainly didn't want to be late. I also didn't want to set an alarm for an early hour since Abby shared my bedroom. This first workshop could be a milestone for me, in more ways than one. Joan would make sure I woke up so I wouldn't be late. I wanted to be able to prove to myself that I could still speak about a subject so intrinsically related to my spouse, as he and I had spent the better part of three months making strategically planned shopping trips in order to prepare the power point presentation. What I didn't tell anyone was that I knew if I stayed at my sister's house, with their bedroom being at the other end of the house from the guest room, I would finally be able to sob with abandon, not having to worry how it might affect my daughter.

I needn't have worried about either the lack of a malfunctioning internal alarm nor an emotional meltdown. Not only was I the first one up at Joan's house, I hadn't cried myself to sleep either. I also managed to do my presentation without a hitch. Joan stayed in the room for moral support in case I faltered, but once I began my well-rehearsed script I easily cracked jokes and laughed along with the attendees. I was amazed that I could operate on auto-pilot even while I was feeling as though I was moving through a foggy haze.

The next month I conducted two "Beginning Writing for Publication" workshops at the River Lights bookstore in downtown Dubuque. At one time, the building had been a grocery store, with an apartment above it. In the winter of 1959, a couple living in that apartment gave birth to their seventh child. That child was me. As a little girl, I had aspirations of being a writer, but in my wildest dreams I could not have imagined that someday I would be teaching writing workshops in the bookstore located below the apartment where I'd lived as an infant. Driving home from that last workshop, I began crying—not with sadness, but with joy. I credited God and my mother for leading me down the path of teaching and speaking engagements, and David for becoming the "wind beneath my wings."

When my mother had passed away, it felt as though she'd left a legacy of creativity behind. It wasn't long after her death that I began writing human interest articles for a local newspaper. Initially very shy in approaching strangers to interview, I decided I would approach each person as though I was my mother. I'd always admired how she could meet a stranger and strike up a conversation wherever she went. I made a conscious decision to become more like her in that respect. The tactic served me well. By approaching others as if each of their lives had merit, I was often able to discover the stories behind the stories.

I also made a decision to attend my first writer's conference because of my mother's notebooks, the words "Utilize your God-given talents," echoing in my head. Attending a writer's conference seemed like a good step towards following my dream of having a book published. My first writer's conference was a Christian writer's workshop held in Cedar Falls, Iowa, the town where David and I had met.

It was with some trepidation I approached the doors of the big white building where the workshop was taking place, not knowing what to expect. *What will this group of so-called Christian women writers think of me? Will I fit in? Am I really welcome, or will they judge me in some way? Are my clothes all right? My hair? Will they find me lacking in some way? Whisper behind my back?*

It was as if I'd regressed to my elementary school years where, because of my obvious poverty, I'd endured several years of intense and merciless bullying, with some of the worst perpetrators being "good little Christian girls." I'd been sneered at, shoved against the wall, tripped, spit on, and called names. *"Peter-Potter, toilet water,"* I could almost hear the echo of those taunts from long ago, taunts that referred both to my surname and a bad septic system that regularly overflowed onto the gravel road in front of our house, despite our use of an outhouse. *Would these "good Christian women" just be grown-up versions of my childhood tormentors?*

Instead, what I experienced inside that building was a workshop rich in spirituality and creativity, and women who exuded a kind of genuine goodness I mistrusted initially. It slowly dawned on me in those three days that the women, and a few men, were some of the most "real" Christians I had ever met, and many of them became fast friends—friends who were there for me after David's death.

That fall, with encouragement from a spouse who promised to hold down the home front, I'd attended my second Christian writer's conference. A speaker there reiterated the importance of stepping through the doors that God opens for us and establishing ourselves as an expert in our subjects. After that conference, I began conducting couponing and writing workshops as a part of my platform building, discovering my true forte. I realized that next to writing, I loved public speaking, which was something my father had foreseen years earlier when I was a very verbal teenager. He'd always advised me to use my talents of writing and speaking for "good, not evil," long before I realized I actually possessed either talent. In fact, I enjoyed doing the workshops so much that after my initial coupon workshop in mid-November, I commented to the co-ordinator in the parking lot that I couldn't believe I was going to be paid to have that much fun. Two months passed before I realized they hadn't actually paid me! I can't imagine any other job I would love so much I would fail to notice I hadn't been compensated.

On the evening of David's wake, I received word that I'd won a Cecil Murphey scholarship to attend what would be my third writer's conference. While my initial reaction was that I couldn't possibly leave my children so soon after their father's death, the timing of the announcement and the fact that it would end on what would have been David and my thirty-third wedding anniversary led me to believe I was meant to attend.

As part of my win, Cecil Murphey sent me a free copy of his book, *Knowing God, Knowing Myself*, a powerful book to read during a period in my life when I struggled to discover who I was without my husband and as I continued down a path of creative growth.

I added quotes from the book to my journal, words that reiterated the importance of following our passions:

> Find the things about which you are passionate. We can give ourselves to enjoying those tasks, jobs, or professions. If we don't find pleasure in what we're doing, maybe we need to think about doing something else. I found my greatest joy in writing; others have experienced joy in other areas.
>
> I want to give you permission to dream—just as I gave myself the freedom to do that. Think passionate and powerful thoughts about your life. Enjoy the excitement that comes when you throw your energies into a project. Why not do your best, regardless of how things turn out? (page 12)

Permission to dream. Passionate and powerful thoughts. Those were words I needed to read as I struggled to discover who I was without

David. I, too, found my greatest joy in writing. And despite everything that had happened, despite the loss of my beloved spouse, I dared to dream of a future, a future without David. With each class I conducted, along with success in my writing endeavors, I felt stronger. Not only was I following my inner desires and learning to live without my spouse, I was actually discovering who I was. I was following my twin passions of writing and speaking, and finding joy in the process. *This is what I want for my children*, I marveled. *What my mother wanted for her children. What David saw happening in me when he'd commented, "You're soaring. You're flying."*

Yes, there was a continual pain of loss, a yearning for the companionship of my beloved David, and a bittersweet sadness with each success that wasn't shared by him. But there was also that small but undeniably growing sense of excitement, too.

What did God have in store for my future?

Driving Miss Mary

If ever there is a tomorrow when we're not together, there is something you must always remember. You are braver than you believe, stronger than you seem, and smarter than you think. But the most important thing to remember is that even when we're apart . . . I will always be with you.

—Winnie the Pooh

"Don't make any major decisions or large purchases for at least a year," I heard from more than one concerned friend or family member. The subsequent nods of my head suggested I was in agreement, even though I was scouring Craigslist for vehicles. It was not a question of whether or not I was going to ignore their advice, but how soon.

It had not been like David to purchase something as expensive as the snow blower he got me for my birthday the previous November. It was also uncharacteristic of him to give me flowers that last Valentine's Day. But what had really surprised me had been David's declaration in the months preceding his death of how he was going to purchase a newer vehicle for me. Never before in our marriage had he mentioned such an intention. Vehicle decisions had always been a shared decision. As recently as the fall of 2011, he'd seen no reason to replace either of our two ancient vehicles. When I'd broached the subject and suggested we use some of the money from the sale of my mother's house for a newer vehicle he'd insisted that the van was just fine, and we didn't need anything else.

David liked nice cars. He loved going to car shows and he had a healthy admiration for other people's vehicles. Yet for his sixty years on earth, he never owned anything particularly nice and definitely nothing "newer." We'd always paid cash for our vehicles and never more than $1500. In fact, the van I'd been driving for over four years cost us a whopping $800. When someone rammed into it while I was parked at a garage sale, their insurance company considered it totaled, paying us $1200 to repair it. Which, of course, we hadn't done.

In our thirty-two years of marriage, we had driven an assortment of older vehicles, including a car that necessitated a good smack with a hammer when it wouldn't start, and a van I once had to duct tape the running board to the side in order to drive home. One particularly reliable car we affectionately dubbed "rust bucket" for its appearance. David got attached to each of these vehicles, always hesitant to get rid of even the most decrepit. It speaks volumes of the male who did not obtain his sense of manhood from the car he drove. David and I had often shared an amused glance between us when others talked about their vehicles as though they were idols. We knew what was really important in life, and it wasn't the things that we owned. David's experience with cancer made that fact all the more apparent. It would be the legacy of the people we left behind that mattered, not the material items we managed to accumulate. David left behind a rich legacy in his eight children and a loving wife who mourned him, not to mention siblings and friends whose lives he had also enriched.

Sometime during the winter of 2011, however, he began saying, "I am going to buy you a Ford ——." It would have been nice if I'd actually listened to my husband, but frankly, I thought he was just dreaming out loud. I did wonder on occasion why he continually said *I am going to buy you* instead of *we will buy*. He expressed his intention often enough that I had finally commented, "I don't even know what vehicle you're talking about," and he replied that it was a smaller SUV. When I informed him it didn't sound very good on gas mileage, he'd maintained that it would be better than the van, and "safer for your traveling." It didn't occur to me then, but after his death I had to wonder why he had suddenly become concerned about my travel safety when he had been driving me every-where: to all my workshops, speaking engagements, and meetings.

After his death, I asked my adult children what vehicle their dad had been mentioning. Though they all agreed it was some sort of Ford, they hadn't listened any better than I had. I was fairly certain the Ford vehicle he'd been talking about started with the letter *e*. I knew what a Ford Explorer was, but I at least knew it wasn't that. After some research on the Ford website and a few pointed conversations, I was confident David had been talking about a Ford *Escape*.

I'm not sure why I made the radical decision to purchase a vehicle on my own, without much input from my adult sons. Yet that is what I purposely set out to do. David's life insurance policy meant not only was I able to pay off the funeral bill, but there was enough left over that I could consider a newer vehicle purchase.

After a few failed Craigslist contacts and test drives, I decided to go through a dealer, something David and I had never done. Because of my Craigslist search, I knew the average price of a used Escape, so I avoided any nearby car lot where the prices were exorbitant. I researched online until I found a dealer that had three Ford Escapes in my price range, and I set up a time to test-drive all three.

When I arrived at the car lot with my two youngest daughters, things began to get a little strange. Despite our appointment, the original salesman I'd contacted wasn't available. Neither were the three prom-ised Escapes. Instead, there was one Ford Escape on the lot and a young salesman named Dan who had been thrust into the role of selling to me. I ended up spending several hours with this young man, including a test-drive where, against all advice from my sons and any common-sense, I followed my heart and divulged everything: the recent death of my husband, the life insurance policy, even the saga of previous vehicles that had included duct tape and a hammer. The poor young man didn't know what had hit him. Struck speechless for a moment, he hesitated briefly before turning to me and informing me exactly what I should be looking and listening for when test-driving a used vehicle. He encouraged my decision to take the vehicle to a mechanic and promised to get me the best deal he could.

After a detailed inspection, the mechanic (who David had always trusted) informed me I was getting a good deal. "Offer them five hundred dollars less," he advised. Once again I completely ignored sage advice and began negotiations at two thousand dollars less than the sticker price. My two daughters raided the car dealership's snack bar and watched television as the young salesman and I sat at a desk alternately haggling and then confiding, for the entire afternoon. My heart warmed towards Dan when I discovered he was the father of a little girl he lamented he didn't see often enough since his divorce. His eyes lit up when he talked about an upcoming wedding in which he would have his first opportunity to dance with the three-year-old. We talked in between each offer I put on the table that he then took to his superior.

"You're dealing with a coupon queen," Dan finally informed his boss when I continued to push for a better deal. All along, during the entire lengthy transaction, I felt as though David were at my side. I pondered many things during the five hours Katie, Abby, and I spent at the car dealer and the mechanic's. I contemplated how this vehicle purchase would be "no big deal" for the average American. That thought was immediately followed by the realization of just how big a deal it would have been for David. He'd never owned a vehicle so new, so nice, or so costly. *It isn't fair! He should be here!* And yet, even as I contemplated that, I knew the only reason I could purchase the newer vehicle was through the loss of David. I was reminded of how often David would inform me, "You deserve it," even when he had a difficult time thinking the same for himself.

"You certainly are composed while you talk about your husband and what he wanted for you," Dan marveled as we waited my turn for the paperwork to be completed after we'd agreed on a price that was substantially discounted from the original selling price. I was equally amazed at my composure and ability to haggle. *Eight weeks, and I'm already able to discuss my marriage and my husband without crying.*

When I got into my newly purchased vehicle with Katie and Abby, there was a thank-you note on the seat from young Dan along with t-shirts emblazoned with the dealership name and some drink cozies. "I never once felt like I was selling you this vehicle," he'd written. "It was as though your husband did all the selling for me."

Tears began flowing as I drove home. Halfway there I had to pull over to the side of the road to compose myself. Soon I was sobbing in earnest, my two girls completely silent in the back seat.

David had indeed bought me a Ford Escape.

Grave Decisions

It's so curious: one can resist tears and 'behave' very well in the hardest hours of grief. But then someone makes you a friendly sign behind a window, or one notices that a flower that was in bud only yesterday has suddenly blossomed, or a letter slips from a drawer . . . and everything collapses.

—quote from French writer, Colette

After graduating from high school in May of 1978, I headed to Cedar Falls, Iowa, to earn money for college. I was a waitress at a Sambo's restaurant, and David was a regular customer, a student at UNI, the college I'd be attending that fall. He was one of our "coffee customers," coming in a few times a week to sit at the front counter and drink copious amounts of coffee while sneaking in some conversation time with the waitresses. I'm not sure why, because I'd never done it for another customer, but one day when I waited on him, I gave him a free slice of pie along with his coffee. He promptly asked me out, later claiming it was an attraction to my legs, but I still think it was the pie.

He followed me back to my brother's house, where I was staying for the summer. I gave him the bacon, lettuce, and tomato sandwich I'd ordered as the free meal I was entitled to on my shift. He ate it in his car while I changed from the ugly starched white uniform, equally horrendous white pantyhose, and nurse shoes into jeans, a comfortable top, and sandals. He took me to a bar in the mall, where we shared a beer and a basket of the free tortilla chips and salsa that was at every table. (*free pie, free BLT, and free chips—was there a pattern here?*) We roamed the mall, stopping to see a visiting petting zoo, where his little finger grazed mine as we simultaneously put our hands on top of the fence to peer over the side. Sparks flew. His pinkie finger grasped onto mine, and we walked through the mall that way, not quite holding hands, but close enough.

Embers restaurant was our next stop, for coffee, a shared salad, and hours of animated conversation. After that, we drove around Cedar Falls looking for a cemetery. Why? Because when David asked me what I wanted to do, for some inexplicable reason I told him I wanted to walk with him through a dark cemetery. We never found the cemetery, but we did walk up and down the dark alleys of Cedar Falls, sharing our first kiss and stopping to swing on a tire swing in someone's back yard.

The summer before his death, David and I had relived some of our college days, driving through the UNI campus, visiting the married student housing complex where we'd spent the first years of our marriage, and searching for the alleys we'd walked on that first date. Sambo's and Embers long gone, we ate at a Hy-Vee deli instead.

"Why did you want to find a cemetery on our first date?" David asked me over lunch. I didn't have a real answer.

"It sounded like fun," I laughed as I shrugged my shoulders, amused that it had taken him thirty-three years to ask that question.

I couldn't have imagined that thirty-four years after that search for a cemetery, I'd be walking up and down rows of tombstones and snapping photos of those that appealed to me. Purchasing a different vehicle was only one of the many big decisions I had to make without my spouse. After the immediate decisions about David's funeral and burial, there was the headstone to consider.

The small metal funeral home sign labeling David's burial plot soon became the bane of my existence. Every time I drove past the cemetery, and with each visit, I couldn't help but think that it looked as if no one loved the man buried in that plot.

My first visit to a monument company had ended with me breaking down in tears, and Sue, the co-owner, gently informing me I was not ready to make this kind of decision. I'd had no idea what I wanted when I walked into that office, nor had I imagined the wide variety of shapes, sizes, and colors of headstones available. I alternated between wishing someone else would make the choice and wanting to be the only one who did so. I desperately wanted to *be* someone else, not a fifty-two-year-old widow having to make this kind of choice. My second visit went a little better. I managed to decide on the size during that meeting and order a cement base. At least the girls and I wouldn't have to visit a plot of grass with a metal funeral home sign sticking out of it. Instead, we would be visiting a cement base where Abby could leave the trinkets she stocked up on "for Daddy" at every garage sale.

The weight of having to choose and order a gravestone was heavy on my shoulders. Each time I drove past the monument office and failed to stop, the anxiety mounted. Ordering a headstone would be my final step in taking care of all the details that burying a husband entails.

"This is for you, the widow," Sue told me during my second visit, when I'd confided that some of my children weren't sure of the ideas I'd shared. "When you're gone, they can argue about it." My son had grimaced with obvious dismay when I'd mentioned I was considering adding a photo from a Chuck E. Cheese visit smack dab in the middle of the stone. Sue's comment amused me as I imagined my son sneaking into the cemetery with a chisel to remove it.

On July 27, 2012, four months after David died, I visited the local monument business for the third, and final, time. The significance of the date did not escape me. The next day would have been thirty-four years since our first date and my long-ago wish to visit a cemetery.

This is for me. And David. I reminded myself when I handed over the single photo David and I had always managed to agree on: one taken in a Chuck E. Cheese photo booth, the same photo I'd submitted to a newspaper for our thirtieth anniversary. David had enjoyed the many compliments he'd gotten at work after the announcement appeared in the paper, knowing it was a private joke between us—the photo had cost a quarter.

"Do you want to pay this off in installments?" Sue asked after she'd tallied up the cost of my choices, with an additional one hundred and eighty dollars just for the black-and-white picture that meant something to me and the man who could get enjoyment (and a wife) out of a free piece of pie.

"No, I'll pay for it in full," I replied as I wrote out the check for an amount that would have horrified my husband. I immediately felt as if a great weight had lifted off my shoulders. The last loose end taken care of—Voilà!

Now all I had left to do was figure out a way to live the rest of my days without the love of my life.

Grief at Twenty Weeks

Blog post on August 14, 2012

I know that more than one widow has been reading my blog, many of them just a few weeks behind me in the grieving journey. If I were to tell the truth, would it scare them?

"Tell the truth." That had always been simplistic advice of my husband. "Just tell the truth."

Really? Tell the truth, that twenty weeks after my husband's death, it hurts more some days? That the reality of my loss has hit home, and the pain cuts even deeper? Does any widow just beginning her journey really need to hear that?

Tell the truth.

The truth is I'm not sure I can continue to do this. It hurts too much. I never imagined this kind of pain. I want it to go away. I want to feel joy, to be happy again. I'm a horrible mess of a mother who smiles and laughs, but rarely does either reach her eyes. I don't want to cook because my husband isn't there to eat, so my biggest accomplishment is a Sunday meatloaf for my older children. I forget things. I've dropped the ball so many times on so many things, in so many ways, letting others down. My eyes well up with tears at odd and inopportune times: in the aisle of the grocery store, at the library when I spot the history magazine David loved so much, while riding my bike because he always rode with me, during a preview for a movie we were looking forward to seeing together, when certain songs play on the radio, even when I hang out the laundry because he'd usually come out and help me. I cry in the parking lot of the grocery store, closing my eyes and leaning my head on the steering wheel to wildly sob. At night, when I lay down and my head hits the pillow, pain wells up inside me and tears form rivulets down my cheeks, wetting my pillowcase. It hurts so much that it aches deep within me. I miss him so much. I am desolate. Bereft. I want to be happy again.

And yet.

Tell the truth.

I continue conducting couponing and writing workshops and become excited, even animated while presenting them. I revel in the public speaking engagements. I enjoy writing the weekly newspaper column my husband was so proud of me obtaining. I haven't missed a week. I have laughed, uproariously, while watching a movie with my children and noted their surprised, but pleased, glances in my direction. I have enjoyed many cups of coffee or lunches with a sister or friend. I've relished the newfound relationship with a son who now reaches out to hug me after each visit and a tween who occasionally grabs my hand on the way into church. I've started bicycling again. Sometimes, I experience a wild surge of joy, an increased appreciation for life in the face of David's death, and wondrous awe in the beauty of nature. I am eager to hone my craft by attending writer's conferences and a monthly writer's group, things David would want me to continue. Sometimes I hear the whisper of a flame inside of me and realize I do have a future, even without David. Before I allow myself to feel guilty for thinking that way, I am reminded of how much he enjoyed seeing me happy, and I can actually smile. Imagine that—smile and feel joy, only twenty weeks after the death of my spouse!

Tuesdays With Mary

Death changes us, the living. In the presence of death, we become more aware of life. . . . It can inspire us to decide what really matters in life, and then to seek it.

— Candy Lightner, founder of M.A.D.D.

Reminders of David were everywhere I looked: that kitchen light I refused to turn off, the cologne bottles and jars of coins on the top of the dresser, and the closet door where his baseball cap hung on the doorknob along with several of his belts. Not to mention the inside of the closet we'd shared, with my favorites of his shirts still on hangers, pushed to the far side. I saw them every time I reached for one of my tops.

After his death, I immediately emptied out David's underwear and sock drawer, offered his jeans and shoes to my sons who wore the same size and took boxes of clothing to my sister's consignment store. I'd also emptied my own drawers of sexy lingerie. Who would I wear it for? But I left one drawer full of t-shirts, along with his wallet and the Iowa Hawkeye pajama pants he'd died in. Just that one drawer, and those shirts still hanging in my closet.

Even the wall calendars in the house reminded me of David. For several weeks after his death, Tuesdays were simply a reminder: the reminder of a Tuesday loss. I brought my husband home from the hospital on a Friday. The following Tuesday I found him unresponsive in his chair. Each week I would count the Tuesdays without him; one, two, three, four, five, six, seven . . . until one Tuesday, I just couldn't bear to keep counting. Tuesday had become an unbearable reminder of a life without David.

Approximately twenty weeks after David's death, I made a conscious decision to stop wallowing in my tears every Tuesday morning and start doing something outside of myself. David wouldn't have wanted me to continue the Tuesday morning countdown, and frankly, I was sick of it. I wanted to use my pain, not let it overshadow my life. Around that same time Shelly Beach, one of the Christian authors I'd met at that first Cedar Falls writer's workshop, asked me if I would consider writing several devotions for a grief Bible. Shelly had become both a friend and a mentor in the world of writing and publishing. Not only did I want to please her by taking on the assignment, I knew it would be a good way for me to delve into the Bible.

While I'd been jotting down Bible verses for this grief Bible assignment, I'd starred this one in my journal:

> Two are better than one, because they have a good return for their work. If one falls down, his friend can help him up. —Ecclesiastes 4:9–10

How could I use my pain to help others? I'd felt foolish as soon as I'd confided to someone that I wanted to help others who were grieving, when I knew I hadn't gotten through grieving myself. Still, I knew grief could be an impetus to action. I'd heard of people who used the pain of loss as an impetus for doing something outside of their own self: M.A.D.D. founder, Candy Lightner, whose thirteen-year-old daughter was killed when a drunk driver struck her from behind as she was walking to a church carnival; Marc Klaas, who founded the Polly Klaas Foundation after his daughter was murdered. Then there was Reve and John Walsh, whose son Adam was murdered in 1981. Reve began the National Center for Missing and Exploited Children, and John became a host of television's *America's Most Wanted*.

Mine was a less shocking loss, but a loss nonetheless. But what could I do besides write blog posts and eventually a book that might help others who grieved the loss of a spouse? I hit upon an answer to that when a box arrived on my doorstep from David's sister Susan: a care package with chocolates, a book, and a water bottle in it, along with an encouraging note. That package brightened my entire day, my week even, knowing someone cared about me enough to have gone to the effort of purchasing things with me in mind, packing them up, and mailing them. Getting something other than bills in the mail had always been a highlight of my week. During those early days of marriage as a refunding/couponing wizard, my mailbox was full mostly of checks and premiums from company manufacturers. I then acquired pen pals through magazines like *Women's Circle*. Though most of those pen pal relationships had been abandoned long ago, I could still count on my friend Mary for regular letters. Sometimes we would write three or four letters in one week. I considered the joy those letters brought me, knowing that if my day was brightened by a card or letter in the mailbox, the same could be said of others. So, I hit upon a solution to my Tuesday dilemma: I decided that every Tuesday I would send at least one card, a letter, or even a package to someone. Instead of focusing on my pain, I would reach out to others.

It was one of the best decisions I'd ever made. Each Tuesday, instead of dreading the day, I'd wake up with anticipation. Who would be the recipient of my outreach that day? One day it was a widow I'd recently met. I chose a beautiful card and wrote that I was thinking of her and praying she was doing well. I stamped the card and added it to my mailbox, unaware that she was in the hospital, having nearly died over the weekend from a bleeding ulcer. Another day the recipient was the sister-in-law who'd sent the box that inspired my Tuesday ritual. Then David's older brother, Keith, was the recipient of a long overdue thank-you regarding his support during David's cancer six years before. My two writing mentors got regular letters. I found that it was much easier to write sentiments I'd always had difficulty verbalizing: *Thank you. You meant so much to David. David loved you. I don't know what I would do without you. I love you.* As I did so, I considered what kind of person David had become after his cancer experience: demonstrative, effusive in his compliments, at ease in saying things like "I love you."

When I began conducting my Tuesday ritual of reaching out to others, I had no idea that someday that ritual might involve another mentor in a very tangible way. Not only had I won a writer's conference scholarship from the esteemed Cecil Murphey, I'd had the opportunity to meet him and take workshops from him at another conference. Thanks to my mentors, Shelly Beach and Wanda Sanchez, I'd actually shared a meal with "Cec," getting to know him as a friend. I'd been writing him occasionally on Tuesdays when I heard that his wife had passed away. With that news, the Tuesday morning ritual of reaching out to others took on a whole new meaning. Knowing how painful the reality of loss became after the busyness of funeral planning, I spent several Tuesdays in a row reaching out to a single person: Cec, the man whose writing had been instrumental in my husband's own faith journey, and whose books had meant so much to me after David's death. The tables were turned: now my words might help Cecil Murphey.

Discontinuing that initial morbid Tuesday countdown after David's death and replacing it with a Tuesday outreach left me with a real sense of hope: if I could stop counting the weeks, maybe someday I would stop counting the months.

Five Months

Blog post on August 27, 2012

Five months ago, my husband passed away: March 27, the day before his birthday.

How am I doing? How are *we* doing?

I'm keeping busy. I have workshops and speaking engagements lined up through mid-November. I'm writing again, thank goodness. I wasn't sure I would survive that brief, but scary, interlude when I could not write anything more than my couponing column and blog postings. I have a clear purpose in my current writing project: to study God's word and glorify his name. My children seem to be functioning well, with brief moments of sadness interspersed with their daily activities. Without any formal grief counseling, my youngest, Abby, is doing better. Perhaps it is true that as humans, we are designed to withstand the inevitable losses in our life.

But grief is kind of messy. We never know when it is going to hit, or how.

The other day I went to get my bike out of the garage and spotted a little note taped to the handle bar. "I fixed your front brakes. Be careful when you first use them." A lump formed in my throat. This was something David had always done for me—keep my tires filled, and my brakes working—always concerned for my safety when riding my bike. He was also my companion for the majority of the bike rides. I am ashamed to admit that for three months following his death, I rode my bike with nearly flat tires. It was my oldest son, Dan, who had checked the brakes and fixed them, leaving the note for me. He also mowed the lawn and used his Dad's weed-eater to trim around the yard that same day.

I cried for most of my bike ride. It was something his Dad would want him to do—take care of his mother. I sat down on the front porch steps when I got back from my bike ride, and there was Dan striding across the street.

"You made me sad," I said, and he looked horrified.

"Why?"

"Because of the note on the bike. You took care of me. Your dad used to do that. I miss that, and it makes me sad. Thank you for doing that, and mowing the lawn too."

"It made me sad, too, the whole time I was doing it: using his mower, using his weed-eater, using his air-pump . . . " his voice trailed off.

We are still sad. We miss David. But I'm also happy. Happy to have a son who cares about me.

On Saturday my sister and niece took me with them to a thrift store dollar sale. "I'll get your Mom to laugh," I heard my sister Pat say to my son Dan when she came to pick me up.

And she did. I had fun. I enjoyed getting to know my great-niece, Emily, a little better, too, and was surprised and delighted to discover her interest in art.

But I also cried. At the checkout, I noticed a woman putting hangers on racks, setting a vase on a shelf, and doing other things that led me to believe she worked at the store. There in her cart was a big plastic bag full of Littlest Pet Shop toys.

"Will you be putting those out?" I asked her, pointing to the bag in the cart.

"No," she smiled. "I'm buying those."

I felt foolish. "I'm sorry, I thought you worked here. I have two girls who love Littlest Pet Shop toys."

"You can have them."

"No, that's alright. You found them. They're yours."

She insisted I take them, and tears sprang to my eyes as she handed them to me. A now-familiar lump formed in my throat. She was a stranger. She couldn't have known that I wanted to bring something fun home to my fatherless nine-year-old.

The woman watched as I paid one dollar for the bag of toys. "Thank you" hardly seemed sufficient.

"Their dad died in March," I mumbled past the lump, not meeting her eyes. "Thank you." She touched my shoulder lightly and I could hardly bear her kindness. I hurried to the vehicle and angrily swept some stray tears away from my eyes. What was the matter with me, that I couldn't accept kindness without crying? I was amazed by the kindness of a stranger.

An older couple walked past on the sidewalk, holding hands and each carrying a bag from the sale. David and I used to go to sales together. More tears escaped. I busied myself with the writing I'd told my sister I would be doing while I waited.

I've been thinking about the kindness of my son in caring about my safety, and then the kindness of a stranger waiting in line at a Goodwill store. I've reflected on the kindness of another widow who gave me a beautiful table for no other reason than that I wanted it. The woman who handed my brother a carefully-folded hundred-dollar bill at the benefit garage sale he held this past weekend to raise money for my nephew's upcoming cancer surgery. The man who donated a good portion of his Star Wars collection to my grandson while he underwent chemotherapy and a stem cell transplant in the hospital. The friend who takes me out for lunch every month. The sister who invites me out shopping so she can see me smile.

Next time I am tempted to do something nice, I won't hesitate. I'll just do it.

And if an act of kindness results in a few tears, I'll remember this: those might be tears of joy.

Be Still

The best way out is always through.

—Robert Frost

"What are you doing?"

David often asked that question of me when I retreated into my own thoughts, which happened quite frequently. I could easily become oblivious to the world around me when I was reading, writing, or simply thinking about writing. I once attempted to explain to David the running commentary I carried on inside my head ever since I was the little girl walking a mile to parochial school every day.

"I narrate my life in my head."

David tilted his head slightly, looking at me quizzically. For a non-writer and casual reader, he was extremely understanding of my writing foibles. In a valiant attempt to share my passions, he'd ask me to tell him about the book I was reading or the article or essay I was working on. My dear husband wanted to get inside my head right along with me.

In the six years following David's cancer treatment, I'd written daily—each and every day for six years. Then I wrote like a madwoman during the weeks following David's death. Until one July day, four months after his death, I got up and couldn't write. Not a word. This went on for days. Outside of my regular newspaper column and a couple blog postings, I could not write. It was a terrible time for me. I sensed, rather than heard, a distinct admonition to "Be still." Never in my wildest dreams had I ever imagined that God might want me to stop writing for a period of time.

"Be still." "Do nothing." "Listen." I attempted to ignore the stirring in my heart. I forced myself to write what amounted to some very bad prose rather than not write at all.

Please, let me write. I need to be able to write about David, became my wretched plea each morning as I attempted to move past the huge boulder that blocked my path. I'd pick up the few pages of the manuscript I intended to become a book about grieving, yet I had no idea where it was headed. I flipped aimlessly through some anthology submission requirements I'd taken the time to print off, certain I could at least write something about my relationship with David or his death to fit the topic.

"Be still."

I could barely hear the gentle admonition with the cacophony going on inside my head.

"Be still," the voice became insistent.

Finally, I realized I wasn't going to be able to continue to write until I faced the demon haunting me: I needed to stop doing and let myself feel the full impact of my loss.

I remembered the widow who'd warned me not to look to her for help since she'd run away from her grief for an entire year. Wasn't I doing the same thing with my incessant writing; as long as I wrote about David, wasn't I trying to keep him alive?

Around the time of these heart stirrings, I'd begun Martha Beck's book *The Joy Diet* and read this:

> Almost all of us have been assaulted by hurricane winds, rapacious fires, and shattering earthquakes of some sort; we live on that kind of planet. Do you remember the last time your preconceptions were blown to smithereens, your heart burnt to a cinder, your confidence shattered? Look back on it now (or if you're in the middle of it, look around) and see if in the midst of that devastation—right in the center of it—you half-sense something still and small. Listen for it. Beneath, around, even within the cacophonous chaos of your life disintegrating,

something infinitely powerful and surpassingly sweet is whispering to you. It is when all our somethings are collapsing that we may finally turn to nothing, and find there everything we need. (page 12)

It took every ounce of courage I possessed to attempt step number one of Beck's Joy Diet: Do nothing for at least fifteen minutes a day.

Do nothing? My initial reaction was, *what a waste of time!* The irony of that did not escape me. How many times in our marriage had my husband lamented, "Why do you always have to be doing something? Why can't you just relax?" He'd pat the couch next to him, entreating me to join him as he watched something on television. He'd turn as he walked up the stairs for a nap, asking me to lay down with him. Occasionally, I did, but more often than not, I was "too busy." And then, in attempting to deal with the loss of him, I was supposed to do just that? Relax? Do nothing for at least fifteen minutes a day? Beck maintained that to be truly happy, we need to "access a point of perfect stillness" at the center of our being. The concept wasn't entirely foreign to me. It was exactly what I sensed in the admonition to "be still" I'd been hearing. Yet it did not come naturally to me to "be still," for even when my body was at rest, my mind would go a mile a minute. I was well aware that if I finally let my mind rest, the pain might come rushing in. Beck warned as much:

> If you have suffered greatly and not yet resolved your pain, you may find it literally unbearable to become physically still; the moment you really quiet your body, you'll feel the monsters of unprocessed grief, rage, or fear yammering at the dungeon doors of your subconscious mind. This can trigger an intense fight/flight reaction, flooding your body with adrenaline that will render you angry, anxious, or restless, rather than peaceful. (page 17)

And yet, those few times since David's death that I allowed myself to be still, above and beyond the yammering pain thundering around in my chest, I did feel a small sense of something else. "Is it terrible of me to feel that God has something in store for me?" I asked a friend early on in the grieving, when the blessed numbness insulated me from the truth that had begun sinking in and gripping a hold of me—the truth that David was never coming back and I had lost my beloved.

"Is it wrong that amid the pain, I can feel a tiny sense of peace, knowing that God has some grand plan for me? That if I am quiet, and open, I will be able to see the unfolding of that plan?"

After several days of attempting to write past the boulder in my path, I put my pens and paper away and tried beginning each morning with prayer and devotional reading, followed by silence. I sat on the couch, not writing. *Here I sit on the couch, not writing*, I thought inanely.

I spent three mornings in a row attempting just fifteen minutes of silence. It was more difficult than I'd ever imagined it could be. Perhaps those who regularly did yoga or walked alone in nature would find it easier, but I wasn't used to either practice. I'd sit uncomfortably in silence, counting down the minutes. My fingers would itch to be writing, my brain going a mile a minute. My eyelids would twitch as the minutes ticked by slowly. I managed five minutes the first day, ten the next. I wondered if some mindless physical activity might help, so one evening I left the house alone on my bicycle, with a dark stone bird I'd picked up at a garage sale clutched in my hand. Like Abby, I'd been picking up little tokens of love wherever I went, and the bird signified how David had been the "wind beneath my wings." I found myself going faster and faster as I rode toward my destination, my heart pumping with both the unaccustomed activity and anticipation. Tears stung my eyes even before I got there—to the cemetery. I rode across the grass and jumped from the bicycle, dropping down to my knees in front of the gravesite. I rearranged the small statues there to make room for the new bird. I ripped the tall grass from around the base. And then I began sobbing messily, my shoulders shaking, my head bowed and snot dripping down my nose. I wondered at the keening noise I heard before realizing it was coming from my own throat.

"*I miss you, I miss you. I love you*," was all I could manage to say before quieting myself and closing my eyes. The silence was palpable. I stayed like that for several minutes. It may even have been the suggested fifteen minutes Beck advised. I can't be sure. I do know that in that silence, in that heavy stillness next to my husband's grave, with my eyes closed and my heart torn wide open, I heard a very gentle but distinct directive:

Get up. You have work to do.

I got up, rode my bike home, and after nearly three weeks of being unable to write, I wrote.

With This Ring, I Thee Wed

Now join your hands, and with your hands your hearts.
—William Shakespeare

"I feel as though I'm hemorrhaging money," I confided to my brother John when he visited one day, pausing in the driveway to ask about my new vehicle. He laughed, but I was serious.

"How much did you get them to go down?" his eyes softened in sympathy of his sister's predicament. I knew he hated to see me all alone. He probably also wondered why I hadn't asked him for his help; he'd always aided us in our vehicle searches. He must have worried I'd been taken advantage of.

"I can't believe the deal you got," he remarked after I told him, with just enough awe in his voice to gratify me. "That dealer has a reputation for never going lower than five hundred dollars below the asking price. You really know how to bargain."

Bargain, yes. I'd been a bargain shopper for over thirty years. But within six months of David's death I'd breezed through more than half of my husband's life insurance policy. Medical bills, a funeral, the gravesite, a vehicle, and a headstone added up to more than an entire year's income. The spending didn't stop there. I was purchasing new clothing for my speaking engagements and satisfying my twin vices of books and stationery at an alarming rate. Everywhere I went I searched for the next book and the next box of stationery that would finally fill that hole in my heart.

At a Goodwill store just weeks before David's death I'd lamented the lack of vintage stationery—the dearth of paper products in our thrift store adventures.

"No one writes letters anymore," I'd said. "So why don't I ever find vintage paper and stationery here?"

David had just smiled at the simplicity of his wife's desires.

The first time I visited a Goodwill store after David's death, I couldn't believe my eyes as I walked up and down the same aisles he and I had frequented together. At every turn, on nearly every shelf, there was something that caught my eye. That first solo trip, I filled a cart with books on grieving, boxes of stationery, pads of paper, scented candles, and pretty baskets. My eyes practically bugged out of my head when I spotted a flock of small bird statues similar to the ones David had given me the previous Christmas. It was as if someone had personally stocked the shelves with me in mind. I left the store in tears, holding bags of merchandise that felt like gifts from above.

While I'd rarely seen stationery in my thrift store trips with David, after his death I couldn't stop finding paper. There seemed to be no end to the books, cards, and stationery available. And I bought it all. I shopped with equal gusto at my sister's consignment store, picking up butterfly pillows, a hope sign for my front porch, and shoes I imagined wearing with a new dress I'd bought that hung unworn in my closet with the tags still attached because it was too flashy, and at least a size too big.

"It was on clearance, and I loved the colors," I imagined how I'd have rationalized the purchase to my husband. But there was no husband, no one to hold me accountable for the mounting bills or the new clothing tags accumulating on my dresser. Even if someone had questioned my wardrobe upgrade, would they have dared to find fault with a grieving widow?

I pushed the shirts of David's that I couldn't bear to get rid of to the side of the closet and filled hanger after hanger with bright colored tops and dark flyaway sweaters. I couldn't seem to stop buying. Even though everything was clearance priced and technically a bargain, I'd sneak the bags upstairs to my bedroom after each shopping trip. I filled my side of the closet and then David's side, crammed bins and drawers in my office full of pretty paper, and still I felt empty.

It could be worse, I rationalized. *It could be Dooney & Bourke purses or diamond jewelry.* I'd never been a high-maintenance woman, nor had I ever coveted designer purses or expensive jewelry. *Nothing would fill the hole in my heart*, I thought wryly, *not even jewelry.*

I'd begun wearing more jewelry when I started conducting workshops after my mother's death—mostly dangly earrings and long necklaces with funky designs. I'd pick them up at thrift stores and on clearance racks. What I wasn't purchasing were diamonds, bracelets, or rings. I'd never worn a ring outside of my wedding ring.

My heart plummeted each time I woefully considered my wedding ring.

The pang of loss over David was never sharper than that moment when the funeral director had handed me David's gold band at the gravesite burial. He'd made a ceremony of it, pulling it from his pocket and presenting it to the widow with a flourish. My throat filled and I had to catch my breath as I took it: the wedding ring, a symbol of our joined hands.

When does a person take off their wedding ring after the death of a spouse? It was a question I'd pondered as I found myself nervously twisting and turning the rings I'd been wearing on my left hand—David's gold band held in place by my band that had been welded to my engagement ring years before. I'd worn the rings ever since our June 1979 wedding.

One option, of course, would be to continue wearing the wedding ring, as my mother had until the day she died, more than twenty-five years after my father had passed away. My mother also never changed the names in the phone book or on her bills.

I instinctively knew after David's death that I wasn't going to be the widow wearing her wedding ring until her own death. I knew I would remove the rings *someday*, but when? I pondered that for weeks, and then months, as I repetitively twisted the rings on my finger back and forth on my finger. I looked to other widows for my answer, and noted that just as many continued wearing their rings as didn't. I worried. *Would my children think I didn't love their father if I removed my rings too soon?* I thought about conversations David and I'd had in the year before he'd died, talking about whether or not we would remarry if one of us died before the other. Early on in marriage, we'd jealously demand that the other remain single. At some point, though, our joking manner had turned serious. We each realized that we couldn't bear the thought of the other being alone, and lonely.

"Okay, I do want you to remarry; to have someone to cook for you, do your laundry," I'd said pragmatically, adding, "and hug you, hold your hand, and kiss you," knowing how much David enjoyed those activities with me. And then I'd quickly add "But no sex," and he'd join me in uproarious laughter.

Would taking off my wedding ring signify I was ready for another relationship? Would it dishonor David? I'd twist and turn the rings on my finger as I reflected on these things. *Would people think it meant I loved David less than someone who kept their rings on?* I couldn't bear that thought, so I refrained from making a decision at all, simply leaving the rings on.

When I'd begun reading the book *Getting to the Other Side of Grief*, I'd abruptly stopped reading with this paragraph:

> In our culture, wearing the ring on the fourth finger of your left hand symbolizes that the wearer is married or in a committed relationship. When a person does not wear a ring on that finger, other people simply know that the wearer is not married or in a serious relationship. The empty finger does not mean you are necessarily looking for another relationship; it simply means you are not married. And the reality for you as a widowed person is that you are now not married. You may have wonderful memories of that time in your life, but the fact remains that you no longer have that relationship. (page 188)

And the reality for you as a widowed person is that you are now not married. That seemed a bit harsh. The co-author of the book, Susan Zonnebelt-Smeenge, had taken her own ring off right after her husband died, then had both her and her husband's rings reset. She wore the new ring on her right hand up until the time she remarried. Was that something I could do with my ring? The simple decision grew more complex as the months went by.

In the end, I didn't have to make the decision: it was made for me. David hadn't lived to see me sign the book contract for the book he'd encouraged me to write, an ethnographic history of the world of avid couponing and refunding. On the morning of March 8, 2010, he'd informed me that the front page of the *Wall Street Journal* had included an article declaring couponing as the "newest extreme sport."

"What happened to the couponing book you started? You need to finish that book now," he'd said that morning at the breakfast table. I pulled out all my files and read what I'd already written, getting excited about it all over again. It was David who encouraged me that morning and continued to encourage me for the next two years as I wrote and researched. It was David who supported my dream of seeing the book published, a dream that would not come to fruition until August 2013 when the book was released. And David would not be there to see it.

On the evening I had completed the final manuscript to submit to the publisher, I relaxed on the couch with my laptop. Having several writing friends who would understand the importance of the milestone, I typed onto my Facebook wall these dramatic words: *Ready. To. Submit. My. Manuscript.* (The periods meant to emphasize the drama). When my finger hit the "Post" button I heard a distinctive "ping" come from the direction of my left hand, and felt a small pain in my finger. Looking down, I realized the pain was coming from my ring that had just cracked in half. In disbelief, I took it off, scrutinizing it carefully. My ring had just cracked, for no reason, and without any provocation, right after I'd announced the completion of my manuscript.

This is it. Time to make a decision about the wedding ring, I thought, and tears sprang to my eyes. I looked at my hand from all angles, reflecting. It was not an old hand, but neither was it a young one. I did not feel married, but neither did I feel single. I was lonely, but not ready to date.

"When do you take off your wedding ring after the death of a spouse?" I posted on Facebook, followed by the announcement that my ring had just cracked in half. Answers ranged from "Never" to "Fix your ring," to "Make a new ring out of it," to the wise, "Whatever feels right." The problem with asking such a question was that I might not like the answer I heard from people I cared about—people whose advice I respected. What would my friends and family think? Would they judge whatever choice I made? It was not likely I'd have the ring repaired. I moved both rings to my right hand, testing that option, but the wedding ring was much too tight on that finger, and I could feel the sharp edge of the crack dig into my skin.

Before I went to bed that night, I put my wedding ring in a small leather bag that held a necklace my father had given me for my sixteenth birthday. Then I fell asleep with David's ring on my right hand, knowing I would have to make a decision soon; the ring was too loose to wear alone.

The next morning I picked up *Getting to the Other Side of Grief* again, continuing to read where I'd left off.

> If you've not made a decision about removing your wedding ring from the fourth finger of your left hand, now may be an appropriate time to do so. The wedding ring is a symbol of a marriage—a union and commitment between two living persons. That commitment ended with the death of your spouse. Removal of your ring as that symbol is a mark of a healthy transition toward moving on. (page 190)

A healthy transition. Moving on. That morning I took off David's ring and added it to the small bag, realizing the tears I'd shed the night before had not really been about removing my ring, but more about the bittersweet reality of what the removal of the ring signified. I was moving on, without David.

That might be healthy. But it was still very sad.

Dream a Little Dream

Blog post on October 21, 2012

Please tell me I'm not the only one who does this: dream about something they'd done during the previous day or will be doing the next day. When I used to do pricing for hours at my sister's consignment store, I would sometimes dream that night that I was pricing more. When my husband and I attended book sales, my intensive searching went on through the night in dreamland. And those few and far between double coupon shopping trips I took with my husband? They, too, were repeated in my dreams. Occasionally, I would have the most amazing shopping trips in my dreams *before* the book sale, bag sale, or double coupon trip, making the actual shopping trip the next day a bit of a disappointment in comparison.

I began the arduous task of revising, editing, and completing my coupon book last night, writing for a good two hours. Considering I haven't touched this book since David's death nearly seven months ago, it was somewhat disconcerting to read references to our shopping trips "We each grab a cart . . . " "When David and I shop together . . . " Repeatedly I had to change David *does* or my husband *will*, to David *used to* and my husband *would*. I went through the entire manuscript, making those kinds of changes, becoming increasingly agitated. David was a huge part of my life, and for the last few years, my usual shopping partner. It is no wonder I still can't get through a grocery store without my eyes tearing up and occasionally crying in the parking lot.

I may as well not even have gone to bed at all last night because my writing continued on well into the night, through my dreams. Oh what prosaic prose it was as I wrote sentence after amazing sentence, paragraphs I would read aloud to David as he quietly sat there smiling. For David did appear in my dream, though he never spoke a word. Judging from his beaming smile my words were very pleasing—quite genius, in fact. Too bad I woke up and couldn't remember even one choice sentence.

The thing is, David often did sit quietly as I wrote, either at the kitchen table, in the chair next to the couch, or when we traveled together. I carried my "portable writing kit" when we took a date day, shopping out of town. (My writing kit consists of a black bag filled with market submission guidelines and whatever I'm working on at the time.) Sometimes we'd sit companionably silent for an hour or more as I frantically scribbled on a legal pad, intent on completing a column, article, or essay. David was remarkably patient and understanding of the power and the glory of the muse in action. How blessed I was to have a spouse who, despite never having experienced it himself, understood the peculiarity of the writer's mind. Silence was indeed golden, when shared with David.

Of course, just as in reality my writing is often interrupted by children, my grandiose written diatribe was interrupted when, in my dream, my oldest son appeared to remind me I was late for my philosophy class. *2:10*, I remember clearly, glancing at a clock on the wall and somehow knowing I was supposed to be at class at 2:00. I jumped on my bike, pumping my legs hard as I weaved my bike in and out of traffic towards a distant campus before stopping, turning around, and heading back home.

"I decided to drop my philosophy class," I told my son when he approached me, "Because I don't need it or want it, and I've decided I'm not going to do anything I'm not really passionate about."

For the record, I'm not enrolled in any college classes, and if I were to ever take any, philosophy is not one I would choose. But after David's death I did make a conscious choice not to take on any projects or jobs that I wasn't truly excited about. I have at least a temporary luxury of being able to do that. It was shortly after my husband's death that I stood in front of the sink doing dishes, tears pouring down my cheeks. *What am I supposed to do now? What will I do without David?* I wondered, fresh sobs escaping. *What would David want for me?*

I had an epiphany then. I contemplated how supportive my spouse had become of my dreams and passions. He reveled in driving me to meetings, workshops, writing groups, and even a photo shoot with the newspaper I would be writing a coupon column for. He bragged me up to oblivious cashiers who mentioned my coupon savings, proudly informing them I was writing a book as he slung his arm around my shoulders. After his cancer, he didn't care so much about things like proper social etiquette; if he felt like hugging someone, he just did it. He blurted out heartfelt sentiments without embarrassment. Who was I to ask him to tame down the gushing compliments he bestowed upon me? I learned to just smile indulgently and bask in the warmth of his praises. We should all be so lucky to have such a supporter of our endeavors.

David hated to see me accept work assignments I was less than excited about, simply to make money. I made the decision, that for one year, I wouldn't take on any projects I didn't enjoy. And for the most part, I haven't. Now I'm working on completing the book project that David had been responsible for me beginning in the first place. David was the one who spotted the March 2010 *New York Times* article that touted couponing as the newest "extreme sport." On the heels of this project, I have two more new book projects waiting in the wings, along with ideas for future speaking engagements. As painful as it is to go on without David, I can't help but feel a bit of excitement as I follow my passion.

And as I do, I imagine David, sitting quietly, and smiling.

"For I know the plans I have for you," declares the Lord, "plans to prosper you and not to harm you, plans to give you hope and a future."
Jeremiah 29:1

My World Gets Bigger

Tell me, what is it you plan to do with your one wild and precious life?
—poet Mary Oliver

Removing my wedding ring didn't mean I was ready to begin dating again, but I was incredibly lonely, and it was a type of lonely that friends and sisters couldn't alleviate. I'd always wondered at the widow or widower who would date before a year was up, but now I understood the compulsion. I'd had thirty-three years of compliments, come-ons, and companionship from one man, and was suddenly thrust into a world devoid of that kind of attention. It was not a comfortable position.

David had never quite believed me when I'd told him that I harbored no desires for any other man. Oh, I'd had my share of harmless crushes, mostly of the unattainable sort that I'd freely shared with him: the voice of James Earl Jones left me weak in the knees, I was attracted to the mind of the detective played by Vincent D'Onofrio from the *Law & Order Criminal Intent* television show, and I'd always imagined Tommy Lee Jones playing David in the movie version of our life. David and I both agreed Meryl Streep would play me. (We'd looked forward to the upcoming movie *Hope Springs* just for that reason, since Tommy Lee would be playing Meryl's husband.) In real life, however, I was committed to one man—I had, in fact, only been with one man in the Biblical sense.

Which is why, when I had a dream about a man other than my husband less than six months after David's death, I was all the more horrified. Not only that, but this particular man was someone I occasionally encountered in my real life, unlike the Hollywood stars I would certainly never see or speak to in reality.

I woke up from the dream with a start, my cheeks flaming. I felt as though I'd cheated on David—having been caught in the arms of another man. Though I didn't dream about him again, I did see this man several times in the next few days. I carefully avoided eye contact when I saw him. *Would he be able to tell I had dreamt about him? Had he dreamt about me too?* As ridiculous as that was, it wasn't long after that night that he invited me out for a drink.

The prospect both thrilled and terrified me: *Another man found me attractive. Maybe I wasn't destined to be alone the rest of my life.* I wondered, briefly, if dating could be the answer to my loneliness. I knew from my research that it was exactly those who loved being married who would desire marriage again, and a remarriage didn't have anything to do with how much the spouse had been loved. I'd loved David so completely. How could I even imagine dating someone else? As lonely as I found myself, I questioned the advisability of getting involved in a relationship so soon. *Would God bring someone else into my life so quickly?* I wondered. Confused, I prayed for discernment.

Thanks to social media, it wasn't too difficult to figure out that despite his good looks and charm, the man was not the type God would choose for me. Offended by several off-color cartoons he'd shared on Facebook, I said no to the drink and breathed a sigh of relief, feeling as though I'd narrowly escaped succumbing to the danger of a bad decision based on loneliness.

Still, I was lonely. My sisters and good friends were a wonderful support, but I missed the attention of a male.

So God sent me a gay man.

I wrote in my journal that fateful night in October 2012:

> I have seen how God puts the right people into our path at the right time. Timothy is a gift from God—the timing uncanny. I needed male companionship without sexual tension. I needed a creative soul, someone who intimately understood loss. I desperately needed a male friend. And there stood Timothy.

It couldn't have been sheer coincidence that at this loneliest juncture in my life, my need for male companionship would be answered at a Friend of the Library book sale. On the last day of the sale, I manned the checkout table with my friend Sheena.

"Look at this," she said as she handed me a completed membership form. "Here's another writer. He came last night and signed his membership form, 'Poet and Wanderer of the Universe.' You don't see that every day in Manchester. I think you should stalk him on Facebook and see if he'd like to join our November writing challenge."

Sheena and I had challenged ourselves to meet at the library once a week during NaNoWriMo (National Novel Writing Month). When I did, indeed, stalk Timothy on his Facebook page, I immediately noted his "widowed" status. Photos on his page included many that looked like he was involved in poetry readings, an artistic endeavor that immediately intrigued me. I messaged him, asking if he'd like to attend our November writing challenge and mentioning I'd be writing in a coffee shop that evening.

When Tim stopped at the coffee shop to meet me that night it felt as though a missing puzzle piece had clicked into place. We fell into easy conversation, first discussing our respective writing endeavors and then the inevitable topic of our losses.

I had never imagined I might be judgmental of a gay relationship, but then I had never knowingly encountered a person who had been in one. When Tim began talking about his "partner," I wasn't prepared for the sharpness of condemnation that rose in my throat. That condescending attitude was immediately followed by the thought that I had no right to judge. I knew several young couples who lived together (an arrangement I didn't wholly approve of either), and I didn't judge them for their lifestyle. I simply loved them. I could no more judge Timothy's lifestyle than I could judge theirs. As soon as I made that logical conclusion, I was able to relax and just listen to my new friend with an open heart.

"How long has it been since your spouse died?" he asked, and when I replied, his voice dropped an octave and his eyes softened. "Oh, you're still in the thick of it." As we discussed our feelings of loss, I gradually realized his anguish over the death of his long-term partner was no less than my own over the loss of David.

We didn't stop talking for two hours, barely pausing for breath between sentences. The owner of the coffee shop began preparations for closing before I realized how much time had passed. My sixteen-year-old daughter, Emily, who was working at the coffee shop that evening, told me later how much she'd enjoyed seeing me laugh.

Tim would become a close friend in the next months, one who intimately understood both my creative side and the emotional abyss of loss. And my children loved him. The first time Abby met Tim, she plopped down comfortably on the couch next to him, listening intently to our conversation about our mutual love of books. When Tim mentioned an upcoming book sale, I hesitated.

"But I haven't gone to a book sale without David," I ventured. "I think it might be too hard."

"But now you have Tim to go with," Abby piped up, and her eager reply touched me. She missed the mother who enjoyed book sales. She missed having a man around.

So it was Tim that was at my side for my first book sale, sans David. My children were delighted that I had a friend nearby that shared my twin passions of reading and writing, a friend that made me laugh and thought to bring me Amish honey when I got sick that winter.

"Did you ever imagine one of my best friends would be a gay man?" I asked my daughter Elizabeth one morning on the phone. "Or that God would answer my prayer for male companionship this way?"

Elizabeth's reply was enthusiastic: "I want one! I want a gay friend who will help me pick out clothes and decorate my house." Then she laughed at the obvious stereotype. She was thankful that I'd found a friend who would haunt thrift shops and attend a writer's group with me—a friendship that might alleviate some of the loneliness she knew I'd been experiencing.

To Heck With the Holidays

Let him into the mire and muck of our world. For only if we let him in can he pull us out.

—Max Lucado, in "Celebrating Christmas with Jesus"

"Have you gone anywhere yet . . . without?" I knew exactly what the woman across the table meant.

I'd thought the early December evening retreat for grieving spouses would be just what I needed as the Christmas holiday approached. Everyone in the room had lost a spouse. Our eyes would meet across the room or the table, and one tender look would say it all: I know your pain.

"I've avoided two weddings so far, but I did attend one birthday party, in a place he and I had never been together. My November birthday was really hard because he always made it special. But the real test will be my family Christmas party this weekend."

The woman nodded, her eyes filling with tears. "I went to a wedding, but I shouldn't have. It was too hard."

By the conclusion of the evening retreat, however, it was obvious to me that I "fell through the cracks" in widowhood. I was younger than the majority of the widows in the room, older than the three young ones. During the evening, an announcement was made about a group for "young" widows, up to the age of forty-five, and another group in the area for singles, ages twenty and up. I felt as though I couldn't join either; I was older than forty-five, and I certainly didn't yet feel "single."

Later, one of the young widows would invite me to their group "because you have young children, and it's a whole different ball game when you have young children."

Yes, I had young children, and it was for them I decided I needed to attend our family Christmas party, a gathering that, just a year before, David had attended with us. These kinds of thoughts boggled my mind as I looked at the calendar: *A year ago, David was here. A year ago, I went Christmas shopping with David. A year ago I had my beloved. Just one year ago, I was happy. I could not have imagined facing a Christmas without David.*

My November birthday had been difficult enough to get through. David had always made it a special day for me. Knowing how hard it was going to be, I invited friends Lois and Ron over for lunch. We'd met them during David's cancer treatment when the radiation oncologist had introduced us. Ron had just begun the same treatment David was halfway through. They'd become close friends, and we'd occasionally meet for lunch at a Dubuque restaurant. It seemed appropriate to share my birthday meal with them.

We'd gotten through Thanksgiving by doing something unprecedented in the history of our family: we'd gone out to eat at a local restaurant's Thanksgiving buffet. I knew my limits, and despite minor protests from my children, I knew there was no way I could manage our usual sit-down family dinner, or even a pumpkin pie. We'd gone out to eat and returned home for pumpkin pie provided by my daughters.

Now Christmas was approaching. It had always been my all-time favorite holiday—the one I excelled at. But this year, I hardly cared. I decided that attending my extended family's holiday party might be a good way to begin the season properly.

It started out fine: I arrived before my children because I was bringing the coffee pot. My siblings welcomed me with hugs and smiles that meant they understood how I might be feeling, "I understood your Christmas card this year, but if you mail me one like that next year I'm really going to worry about you," my brother John had commented. The card he was referring to was the "tombstone" one I'd sent to everyone on my Christmas card list.

I didn't care if it was a bit macabre. When an online card company advertised a special offer of mailing personalized photo cards for less than the cost of a stamp, I knew I'd discovered my answer to the dilemma of handling my annual Christmas letter and greeting card. In one fell swoop I could design a personalized card, type in the addresses from my address book, and have the company do all the addressing and mailing of the Christmas greeting. But how would I personalize the card? I scrutinized the cheery card designs and the photos I had saved on my computer. What photo embodied my entire year? There was only one. It had to be the headstone that had been completed and installed on my November birthday with the butterfly and words, "Wind Beneath My Wings" above David's name, the Chuck E. Cheese photo of David and me in the middle, and the inscription of my name and date of birth. Macabre, yes, but the only photo that said it all: 2012 was the year I lost the wind beneath my wings, the year my children lost their father. Any other event in the year paled in comparison. I added the photo to the card layout and searched for a meaningful verse to add. I finally settled on my own sentiment: *Live like you are dying! Love with all your heart— laugh, because this is the only card you'll ever get with a tombstone on it.*

"You have no idea how well you are doing," John complimented me just a few minutes after he mentioned the Christmas card. What did that mean: That I was doing well? That I'd come to a family gathering? That I'd remembered to bring food? That I was dressed, and my hair combed? That I was wearing shoes? I wasn't sure, but maybe just making an appearance at a family event meant I was handling things well.

As the room filled with more and more coupled pairs, I began to feel claustrophobic. I forced myself to walk around, clutching a cup of coffee more for emotional strength than sustenance. I'd retreated to a corner near the door when the last sibling arrived. When my brother-in-law Dave hugged me with extra tenderness, my stomach lurched and the room started to spin. As he hung up his coat, I fumbled for the doorknob. Outside, I sprinted towards my vehicle, dumping the coffee in the snow. Within the safe confines of the vehicle, I began sobbing, realizing the mistake of coming without my children. If I'd had the sense to grab my purse before fleeing the building, I would have driven away.

I waited until my children arrived before rejoining my family. No one commented on my red-rimmed eyes, but my sisters stuck close by me. I wondered if Denise was even aware of how she lightly stroked my arm as she talked to someone on the other side of her. I laughed a little, joking that I should have just gone outside and lain down in the snow. My sisters and I chuckled over the imaginary scenario.

"Mary is outside in the snow, making snow angels," one would say as she glanced out the window. She might come outside to join me, commenting wryly, "That's not a very good snow angel, Mary. There are no wings," as I lay curled up in the snow in a fetal position.

Ironically, by late afternoon, as my sisters and I settled at a table full of photo albums, I no longer wanted the party to end. I'd needed my sisters' support and craved some normalcy. My children left before I did. I wanted to sit with my sisters, drinking coffee, and pretending everything was fine, for hours. Or maybe forever.

I didn't want to go back home where my children sat, waiting for permission to eat the chili I'd had the forethought to throw in the crockpot. (Was that doing well?)

When it was apparent that the party had, indeed, ended, I bolted out the door again, without saying goodbye to anyone. I cried in my vehicle as I headed to the cemetery, cried as I walked through the snow in ridiculously inappropriate sandals, and cried some more as I knelt in front of the tombstone, bowing my head and laying my hand upon the frigid stone, and then tracing the image of David's face with a numb finger.

"Have you gone anywhere yet . . . without?"

I did, and I survived. Perhaps that meant I was doing well.

The First Christmas

Then she saw a star fall, leaving behind it a bright streak of fire. "Some-one is dying," thought the little girl, for her old grandmother, the only one who had ever loved her, and who was now dead, had told her that when a star falls, a soul was going up to God.

—Hans Christian Andersen, *The Little Match Girl*

"Mom, why are you sleeping again? You're starting to scare me." My daughter's gentle, but urgent voice startled me awake. The concern on her face was obvious.

The booklet the funeral home sent me on grieving through the holidays had suggested taking naps as a form of self-care. I'd never been the napping type, but I was willing to try anything to get me out of the funk I'd sunk into. I'd gotten through the first holiday party, but still had a difficult time facing the prospect of a Christmas without David. I felt panicky; how was I going to get through Christmas? It wasn't like I could skip the holiday entirely, which is what I really wanted to do. I had children to consider. I had a nine-year-old daughter to think about. Didn't she deserve a Christmas?

So I slept. The irony of my taking naps did not escape me. Hadn't I always questioned David's afternoon trysts with the sandman? David was a regular napper, one who'd persistently ask his wife to join him, a request I rarely met. "I have things to do." "Naps don't help me get anything done." "The kids won't let me join you." "I'm not convinced naps even help." "If I'm tired, I'll just drink more tea, another cup of coffee, take a walk."

"Take care of yourself. Do whatever it takes to get through the holidays," the booklet advised. So I'd started napping. For several days, around 2:00 in the afternoon, I pushed back in the recliner, closed my eyes, and promptly fell asleep.

"Mom, why are you sleeping?" my daughter had asked, and I had no real answer. Did I think I could sleep through Christmas? For the kid's sakes, I had to rally, so rally I did.

Despite my looming dread of the holiday, our house began looking quite festive. Rather than use our old tree, I ordered a drastically reduced pre-lit tree from the Internet. Instead of pulling out the boxes of ornaments that would have inevitably reminded me of the years I'd shared Christmas with David, I'd purchased several sets of blue ball ornaments from my sister's consignment store. Our tree was beautifully decorated.

Emily had gotten into the spirit of establishing new rituals, designing Abby's usual red and green countdown chain with a little twist. On each chain, Emily had added something for Abby to do on that day. One day it was "Wave to a stranger." Another said, "Do five nice things for others." Rachel added to our new rituals by spending time with the girls designing a gingerbread house. In over thirty years of Christmas traditions, we'd never had a gingerbread house!

Christmas Eve was bearable only because my daughter Elizabeth offered to host it at her house and my sweet sister Denise, who didn't even celebrate the holiday, offered to be my companion through the evening. Though fewer than usual, there were still plenty of gifts under the tree on Christmas morning. I was so proud of my accomplishment: I'd gotten through Christmas Eve and the morning's usual festivities.

One of my sons had brought breakfast pizzas for us to eat after we unwrapped the gifts, so we really weren't hungry when Ben and Elizabeth joined us after attending noon Mass. I enjoyed watching my grandchildren open their gifts, reveling in their squeals of joy. It was only when I heard one of them comment, "I'm hungry," that it suddenly occurred to me—I'd forgotten all about Christmas dinner! I always cooked a ham, potatoes, vegetables, and rolls, and yet I had none of these things in the house. I felt it then: a looming sense of panic. How could I have forgotten Christmas dinner? What had I thought my children were going to eat?

"I'm hungry," I heard again, in a louder voice, and then a, "Me too."

"What were you going to make for Christmas dinner?" one of my older children asked in a very reasonable tone. I cleared my throat, but couldn't speak. There was no real explanation for my behavior. I'd been so intent on getting through this first Christmas without David. I'd found new rituals to replace the old, wrapped gifts, and even made cutout sugar cookies. I'd modified Christmas in order to endure it. What I hadn't done was plan on or prepare a Christmas meal. Everyone was looking at me expectantly by this point, including my sweet, hungry grandchildren.

"I forgot all about Christmas dinner," I finally admitted. No one batted an eye.

"We can go to Kwik Star and pick up some pizza," my daughter Rachel helpfully contributed. "I'll give you a ride."

I pulled on my boots and bent down to pick up some of the plastic Christmas flowers I'd used for decoration on the baskets I'd given my adult children. Dan eyed me warily, knowing what the flowers were for. "You don't want to go there today."

"I know, but I need to."

Rachel waited in the vehicle while I trekked across the snow-covered grass. *Is there any sadder place to be than a cemetery on Christmas Day?* I wondered. (*Except perhaps Kwik Star?*) I stood in front of David's tombstone, attempting to push the stems of the colorful plastic poinsettias into the hard ground next to the tiny metal tree I'd brought the week before.

"I'm not doing too good without you," I whispered, laying my hand on the top of the cold stone. "I forgot all about Christmas dinner." I could almost hear David's chuckle. "I miss you so much."

"I ended up in the cemetery," I wryly confessed to a stranger in line at Walmart the next morning when she asked how my Christmas had been. I saw her eyes fill with tears.

"Me too."

"Who did you lose?" my voice softened.

"My son. He committed suicide. He left behind a wife and three children."

We continued talking as my purchases were rung up—about the first Christmas, the sadness of ending up in a cemetery on a holiday, and the pain of getting through that first year.

"They tell me it gets better," she said with a sigh.

"Can I give you a hug?" I asked shyly before I turned to go. She nodded eagerly, and one small sob escaped her as I squeezed her shoulders tightly.

I might look back on that first Christmas and remember it as the year I did so many things so badly, the year I forgot to feed my family.

Or I might just remember it as the Christmas I learned what it meant to reach out to a hurting stranger.

A New Year,
Another Challenge

*But grace can be the experience of a second wind, when even though
what you want is clarity and resolution, what you get is stamina and
poignancy and the strength to hang on.*
—Anne Lamott in *Help, Thanks, Wow: The Three Essential Prayers*

Could I consciously decide to have a good year, or did my widowed
status preclude that possibility?

If you'd asked me that question on New Year's Eve, I might have said
my happiness depended upon my situation. Despite the fact that David
and I had never done anything special to celebrate the holiday, I spent a
good portion of the evening wallowing in my widowhood. Most years,
David and I hadn't even stayed up until midnight. Sometimes though,
my husband would get up to go to the bathroom, and if he saw that his
movements had awakened me, he'd eagerly grab my hand in the dark
and whisper, "Happy January First!" He delighted in beating me to that
first day of the year greeting, even extending the game to the first day of
each month.

Because we had failed to celebrate the holiday in any meaningful way,
I hadn't dreaded New Year's Eve. So I was blindsided by the sadness
that enveloped me as darkness fell. In an attempt at levity, I watched
a comedy DVD with Katie and Abby, laughing out loud a few times,
which seemed to please the girls. When they put in another DVD, I
wandered off.

"Whatever you are doing at midnight sets the tone for what you will be doing the rest of the year," one friend had written earlier in the day on my Facebook wall, so I was determined to do something very meaningful like writing or reading. I listlessly flipped through the pages of a manuscript I didn't have the energy to work on. Then I searched my shelves for a fiction book to escape into, but nothing appealed to me. Restless, I ended up on Facebook, where I read the fun-filled statuses of others who were celebrating: planned parties, weekend getaways, or a quiet evening spent with a partner and a glass of wine. No one else seemed to be lamenting the loneliness I was experiencing.

"Happy New Year!" I read repeatedly.

"That's easy for you to say," I grumbled. "You still have your loved one."

I went to sleep before midnight, waking up not long after. Glancing at the clock as I returned from the bathroom, I noted it was 2:00 a.m., the very hour David had greeted me with New Year's wishes just one year before. *"David!"* I stifled one small sob before promptly falling back to sleep.

When I got up that next morning, it was with the acute awareness that I was beginning my first new year in thirty-four years without David. I picked up the devotional my friend Mary had given me for Christmas, reading this Bible verse designated for January 1:

> I am growing and becoming strong in spirit, filled with wisdom, and the grace of God is upon me. —Luke 2:40

I spent some time reflecting on that verse, considering my own spiritual growth the previous year. I wrote in my journal:

> A year ago, I was a different person. I had a spouse I loved very much and a promising year ahead of me with a calendar filled with scheduled activities. I lost my best friend when David died in late March, but I carried on and fulfilled my obligations and added others. I discovered a strength I didn't know I had, and gained something totally unexpected during those darkest of days when I cried out to God and felt the comfort of his care: I found grace.

Could I make a conscious decision to have a good year, despite the death of my spouse? I believed I could *because* of my loss. In fact, I decided that I must. I could use my pain to reach out and help others. I was actually looking forward to a new year and a new start. What I couldn't know was that just one week into 2013 our family would be faced with yet another trial.

I was at my daughter Elizabeth's house on Tuesday, January 9, babysitting my two grandchildren, nine-year-old Becca and four-year-old Joe, when the phone rang. Dan was waiting with me for news from Elizabeth and Ben, who had taken seven-year-old Jacob in for a CT scan. I picked up the phone with trepidation.

"Jacob's cancer has returned. They said there isn't anything more they can do." The anguish in Elizabeth's voice was heart wrenching. Less than ten months after David's death and after more than two years of treatment, Jacob was losing his fight with cancer. For the first time since David's death, I was glad that he was not here to face this reality.

Dan and I couldn't even meet Ben's and Elizabeth's eyes when they returned home with Jacob. What could we say? What could we do? Ben busied himself with setting up a new PlayStation they'd purchased for Jacob on the way home, and Jacob's eyes lit up as he excitedly showed us the games that went with it. I glanced at Elizabeth, quickly looking away when I saw the shattered look in her eyes. She called me on the phone later to fill me in on the doctor's meeting.

The words the doctors had used left me stunned. They took on a life of their own, echoing in my head that evening.

"The news is not good." "No cure." "Chemo for comfort." "Hospice." "Nothing more we can do."

How could this be? Surely there had to be other options. Before I went to bed I made the mistake of searching online for possible answers. Instead, I stumbled upon a website that included a mother's vivid, horrifying description of her son's death from the same cancer as Jacob's. I felt as though I might throw up. My heart caught in my chest. I couldn't breathe.

How can I do this? I'm still grieving David. I can't help my daughter. I can't do this! I wanted to run away. *This isn't fair! We have been through so much already.* I finally fell into a fitful sleep—a sleep of despair—with those words and the image of a dying child in my head.

The next morning my legs nearly gave way as I stood up from the bed; my arms felt weak and my hands shook. What was going on? I'd been so certain of my spiritual strength. I'd sunk all the way to the bottom when I lost David and had gradually been working my way back up. And now this! A dying child. Broken-hearted parents. The loss of a husband was one thing—a personal grief that had cut to the bone. But the loss of a grandchild would mean the reality of a grieving mother and father, an unnatural grief and pain I would have no way of alleviating for my own child. (Children, because Ben is like a son to me.) I felt hopeless in the face of it.

I remembered then the words from C. S. Lewis in *A Grief Observed*:

> You never know how much you really believe anything until its truth or falsehood becomes a matter of life and death to you. It is easy to say you believe a rope to be strong and sound as long as you are merely using it to cord a box. But suppose you had to hang by that rope over a precipice. Wouldn't you then first discover how much you really trusted it. . . . Only a real risk tests the reality of a belief.

Was I strong enough to endure this? Strong enough to help my daughter face what no parent should ever have to face? Did I believe, truly believe, that God was working, even in the face of this? A dying child?

I tugged at that rope of faith that had been weaving itself during the months following David's death. I knelt down and prayed the prayer of a grandmother's heart: "Dear God, give me strength. Give my daughter and the son-of-my-heart strength to deal with this. If there is anything that can be done, please lead us to an answer. Please hold Elizabeth and Ben close to you. Let them feel the prayers of others lifting them even as the words of the doctors pierce their hearts."

I jerked the rope harder, testing my faith. I stepped off the cliff, holding onto God's word with all my might.

And the rope held.

What exactly was it I had lamented in Joyce Carol Oates's *Story of a Widow*? Hadn't it been the lack of hope? How dare I then become hopeless and helpless when my daughter needed me to be strong! How dare the doctors at the University of Iowa shake their heads and murmur words of despair and hand my daughter and son-in-law *funeral papers*!

I turned on the computer with a strengthened resolve, beginning a systematic search for anything that might mean even a slight chance of survival for Jacob—a nugget of hope for his parents.

I spent most of that morning doing research and making phone calls. I'd discovered a hospital and a doctor in Pennsylvania where a clinical trial study was being done for recurring Wilms' tumor. The more I read, the more I believed Jacob could qualify, but I wanted to hear that from the source of the study. I left my name and phone number for the doctor who headed it. I discovered eighty-four hospitals were participating in the study, including the Mayo Clinic. I called Mayo, but was unable to talk to the person heading the study there. Instead, I left all our information and was told that a committee would decide if Jacob was eligible.

In the meantime, I requested prayers from others. Two grandmothers who had lost grandchildren responded that they were fervently praying. Cecil Murphey, who had become both my spiritual and writing mentor, committed to praying for my grandson and his family for one year. People all over the United States were praying after they saw our posting on the "Jacob's Ladder" Facebook page we'd established when Jacob's cancer was initially diagnosed. I felt stronger with each promise of prayer.

Ben and Elizabeth were granted at least a short season of hope when Jacob was enrolled in the Phase II clinical trial at the Mayo Clinic. Elizabeth, pregnant with her fourth child due on what would have been her father's birthday, would need to drive to Mayo weekly for the checkups in this last-ditch effort to stop the growth of the tumors that now invaded little Jacob's lungs.

The previous summer, in the thick of grieving David, barely able to take care of my own children, I was unable to handle babysitting my grandchildren during the forty days Jacob was in the hospital for a stem cell transplant. Instead, I'd arranged for a young girl to babysit. Then I'd studiously avoided little Joe's confused eyes every time I picked up the babysitter and dropped her off at their house. This time around, however, I was determined to do all I could for Elizabeth and Ben, including babysitting my own grandchildren while Elizabeth made the six-hour round trips to Rochester with Jacob.

A Season of Illness

That was the way illness appeared in a house, in the corners, in be-
tween floorboards, on the hooks in the closet, along with the sweaters
and coats.

—Alice Hoffman, *The Third Angel*

The scratchy throat began in the vehicle on the way to Mayo. It rapidly progressed so that I began to feel a bit dizzy as I walked the long halls of the clinic with Elizabeth and Ben. Then came the litany of lab technicians, nurses, and doctors that poked and prodded little Jacob, and with serious faces and gentle words, discussed this last-ditch effort that might buy this little boy some time, or perhaps even bring about a miracle. *Miracle* and *hope* were the two words we clung to in desperation.

By the time we returned home, I knew I was in the throes of a full-fledged illness, one I hoped had not been passed onto Jacob or my other two grandchildren. Illness struck, and it struck hard. I was sicker than I'd been in a long time. The last time I remembered being that ill was in January 2001, when a bout with influenza ended in pneumonia for me because I'd neglected to take care of myself while I took care of everyone else.

This time, however, I listened to my body. For days I did little more than sleep and watch *Little House on the Prairie* DVDs. I slumped on one end of the couch and within days Abby was curled up on the other end with the same symptoms. My friend Tim brought over a huge jar of Amish honey and instructed me to mix it with cinnamon and take it by the tablespoon. I did so, along with copious amounts of tea. My heart ached with loneliness for David: he would have taken good care of me, plying me with sugar/cinnamon toast along with the tea.

While I'd had no fever, Abby registered a high fever, along with the same symptoms as mine: body aches, chills, coughing, sniffling, sneezing, stuffed head, and a scratchy, sore throat. I took her to the doctor, where she tested positive for Influenza B. I swayed a little with this news, and then sat down abruptly, still ill myself.

"Could I have it too?" I asked. "I have all the symptoms but without the fever."

"No, you'd have a fever," the on-call doctor stated emphatically.

This was not true. I discovered later when perusing the Center for Disease Control's website that while a fever is a common symptom, it is not universal. Abby and I had Influenza B and it went through our house like wildfire, even infecting two of my adult children who had visited over the weekend. I was relieved that none of Elizabeth's family got it, despite our close quarters in the drive to and from Mayo.

It broke my heart that I was unable to watch my grandchildren while Elizabeth made the first two treks to Rochester. I felt as though I had failed her once again.

After fourteen days of illness, I began feeling human again. Before I could offer my babysitting services, however, my chest started hurting. For several days, I ignored the heaviness and pain I experienced every time I breathed in deeply. Despite the promise I'd made to myself that I would never ignore the symptoms of a heart attack, I instead waited for the pain to subside. By day four, my son Dan insisted I see a doctor. He took me to an emergency room, where I was immediately hooked up to a heart monitor and blood was drawn. My heart hammered with the memories those steps brought: David in the emergency room being informed he'd had a heart attack, his widened eyes looking to me for reassurance.

"Can Mary drive me?" he'd asked when they told him he had to get to the Dubuque hospital to see a heart specialist. Of course the doctor couldn't allow that, but I was able to kiss David's head before he was taken away in an ambulance. By the time Dan and I had arrived at the hospital, the stent surgery had already been done.

I couldn't help but think how that emergency room visit ended, and though the prospect of joining David sooner rather than later and not having to view the demise of my grandson was somewhat appealing, I suddenly knew I didn't want to die.

I waited until the male nurse sent Dan back to the waiting room before I let myself cry.

"What's wrong?" the nurse asked in obvious concern.

"My husband died of a heart attack last year," I managed to say before the crying resumed. "And I don't want to die and leave my children orphans."

"I don't think you're having a heart attack," he patted my arm.

I insisted Dan return home when the doctor informed us it wasn't a heart attack, but they wanted to keep me overnight for observation and a stress test in the morning.

By the time I was released, the chest pain was joined by a headache, a scratchy sore throat, and the all-too-familiar body aches. I was sick again.

"I think your chest pain was the beginning of bronchitis," the doctor commented as he signed the release papers.

How odd it was to recognize a similar pain I'd suffered. I wrote in my journal the following day:

> Grief is not easy, nor tidy. It does not always come when we are expecting it, nor can it necessarily be anticipated. I was not prepared for the question from the doctor when chest pain sent me to the emergency room over the weekend.
>
> "Can you remember another time when your chest felt like this?"
>
> My fingers splayed across my aching chest as I carefully pondered her question. Then I nodded vigorously as I remembered. Tears streamed down my cheeks unchecked as I whispered hoarsely, "Yes, I do remember. After my husband died, it hurt like this. My chest felt full and heavy, and I thought then, *Oh, this is what it feels like to have your heart break.*"

I did not expect grief to hit again the next morning when the man conducting the treadmill test told me to turn around so he could help me close my gown. No one could have prepared me for the tears that stung my eyes as his fingers brushed against the back of my neck while he clumsily fumbled with the strings. The tender touch reminded me of David, who had done the same thing for me after each of my surgeries.

The bronchial discomfort I was experiencing was eerily reminiscent of the tightened, tear-filled heaviness of a chest that expanded with the breaking of a heart.

The Ides of March

So this was how it was to be, now: I would do my best to live in the
quick world, but the ghosts of the dead would be ever at hand.
                                        —Geraldine Brooks, in *March*

When I'd finally recuperated from both illnesses, it was mid-February
and Elizabeth had made several trips to Rochester with Jacob while Ben
took off work to care for the other two. I was able to watch Becca and
Joe during the remaining appointments, until a CT scan revealed that
one of the tumors in Jacob's chest had doubled in size—he was no longer
eligible for the study. A consult with a doctor at St. Jude's concurred:
there was nothing more do be done. Barring a miracle, it looked like this
cancer wasn't going to be eradicated. Cancer was winning the battle in
Jacob's little body.

Initially, I didn't want to believe that prognosis, certain there had to be
something the doctors were overlooking. I'd surf the Internet for hours,
forwarding Phase I drug studies to Elizabeth, despite her gentle admo-
nitions not to. Both the Mayo and St. Jude's doctors had recommended
against Phase I trials since they were simply testing safe dosages, and
there was no proof of efficacy with the drugs.

Other concerned friends, family, and even strangers were doing the
same thing: e-mailing Elizabeth and Ben with ideas and website addresses of alternative cancer treatments. When the treatment made even
the slightest bit of sense to Elizabeth, she researched it. It soon became
apparent that children were not qualified for many of the alternative

treatments or there was no scientific evidence to support the claims of the various products. At some point, and Elizabeth reached it before I did, the possibility that Jacob was going to die became a reality.

"Don't you believe that Jacob can be healed?" some persisted, pressuring Elizabeth to *believe—just believe—*and Jacob would be healed. The underlying message was that Elizabeth's faith was not strong enough to save her son. I remembered then the same kind of statements David and I had heard when he was undergoing cancer treatment, when several well-intentioned people informed David that all he had to do to rid his body of cancer was to believe he was healed. I'd resented the implications then, and I resented them for my daughter now. People die. Good people like David die too young, and innocent little children die, and the strongest faith in the world cannot keep anyone on this earth forever. If only the same Christians professing their faith in healing could clearly see the flip side of that faith, that earth was not where we ultimately belonged. If Jacob died, he would be going Home.

I stopped pressuring Elizabeth with e-mails pertaining to Phase I trial information. Jacob was not a guinea pig. His little body had been through enough. He was happy not to endure further treatment, intent on spending his days like a normal little boy, playing with his brother and sister and looking forward to a baby in the house. Jacob adored babies.

As Elizabeth's March 28 due date approached, so did the March 27 one-year anniversary of David's death. I felt a real sense of foreboding as everyone who had traveled this path of grief before me had warned how painful the impending milestone could be. At the same time, I looked forward to reaching it. Despite the words of the widows who had continued attending a grief support group years after their loss, I expected the second year of grieving would be easier than the first. I also suspected that the anticipatory grief I was feeling about Jacob was impeding the natural progression of grieving my spouse. There were many days I felt as though I was shutting down emotionally.

Sadness permeated everything I did, and unshed tears were so close to the surface I sometimes felt as though I was choking on them. My emotional nerve endings were so raw, I'd begin crying at the slightest provocation. While this was certainly an uncomfortable state of being, it also gave me an increased empathy. I was feeling compassion and love for others as I never had before.

One way I found to cope with this heightened awareness of the fragility of the human condition was to begin a Bible study. If I'd found healing from the Bible, then surely there were others who needed the same thing. I approached Kathy, the Religious Education Director at our church, about forming a Bible study. She in turn discussed it with the parish priest. The church agreed to pay for the DVD kit if members paid for their own study journal. The priest asked if I would speak in front of our congregation, along with the other two churches in the cluster, detailing my reasons for forming a Bible study and how the Bible had helped me after David's death. So it was that the weekend before what would be the one-year anniversary of my husband's death that I stood at the front of my church and spoke about my loss of David and the power of God's word to alleviate grief. That Saturday evening would be the first time since I'd become a widow that I would remain in the church pew for an entire service instead of leaving early, choking back tears, as I had been doing for nearly a year. Attending Mass had just become an endurance test for me. David had always held my hand in church. Seeing older couples together just reminded me of my terrible loss—David and I would never grow old together.

I spoke at that one Saturday service and rushed from church to church the following morning, speaking at four additional services. When the religious education director had asked how many books she should order, I'd told her maybe ten or fifteen.

Fifty people signed up for that first Bible study.

I'd previewed several Bible studies before choosing one that resonated with me. When the facilitator in the DVD lesson asked: "Do you think that God speaks to you?" I'd begun to cry.

Before David died, I would have said no—God didn't speak to me. But now I knew I just hadn't taken the time to listen. God reached me that July morning when I woke up and couldn't write. He took away my writing and asked me to "Be still." That had been an extremely frustrating and fearful time for me, and it lasted for several weeks.

Looking back, I think it might have been the *only* way God could get my attention. It was during that time that I learned to listen to God. But now, when I really needed to, I wasn't hearing from God at all. Facing Jacob's death was challenging my faith in ways I'd never imagined. I'd been so determined to find the answer to Jacob's survival through Internet searches, not willing to listen to that still, small voice that might be whispering an answer I wasn't willing to hear. *Where are you, God?* I wondered. I yearned for the frequent and tangible "messages from heaven" that Abby and Jacob were the recipients of.

I was jealous of their propensity for finding coins ever since David's death. David loved coins of all kinds. He was one of the few people I knew who would actually stop to pick up a penny. So it had not surprised me that after her beloved father's death, Abby began finding coins in droves everywhere we went.

"That's from your daddy. It means he's watching out for you," I'd say when she'd point out yet another coin on the sidewalk, the floor of a grocery store, or in the library. It was usually pennies, but she'd also found dimes and even quarters. Like her dad, she began stopping to pick up pennies on the sidewalk, even slamming on the brakes of her bicycle one day for a copper circle she'd spotted. You'd think she was finding diamonds by the extent of her joy in the discovery. Once while we waited in line at a Subway, my eyes widened in disbelief when Abby pointed to the floor where a plethora of coins lay in disarray. How could every other customer before us have failed to see nearly a dollar in assorted change?

Jacob was also discovering coins in odd places. Each time he visited my house he'd find stray coins, holding them out in the palm of his hand to show me, a huge smile on his face and delight in his eyes. Even if I'd vacuumed the rug right before his visit, he'd still unearth a dime or a penny in the middle of the floor. "That's from Grandpa," I'd say, and his smile would light up the room. After the Subway goldmine, I couldn't help but believe there was more to the coin discoveries than could be explained away by sheer coincidence or a heightened awareness of loose change. I loved that Abby and Jacob were finding "Pennies from Heaven," even while I'd ached for a similar sign meant just for me. Where were my messages?

During that first Bible study I attempted to explain how God had gotten my attention since David's death, how he'd urged me to "be still" and listen. "If I can do nothing else than help some of you learn to listen, to hear the voice of God, then my purpose for forming this Bible study will be fulfilled. But I am on this journey with you. I think we can help each other out." I knew I would be learning just as much from those who were taking the study as from the study itself.

"We'll be learning together," I confided to the group. "I am humbled to serve as your facilitator."

After the class, I returned to the table of materials, filling a box with the remaining journals and handouts. Tables and chairs were being put away. I was surprised when several attendees stopped on the other side of the table to tell me how thankful they were for the class and to ask about Bibles. I was amazed to realize others needed this just as much as I did. Gradually, the room emptied.

Alone, I closed my eyes for a moment, reveling in the quiet and thinking about what had just transpired in a room full of people who were searching for answers in how to live their life. What an honor to be a part of that! I felt a surge of excitement, even as I ached with sadness, wondering just how and when I might hear from God again. When I turned to get my purse, I spotted it, and my breath caught in my throat: a bright shiny dime lay face down in the middle of the floor behind me, a dime that could not have been there just a minute before, because I would have seen the unmistakable beacon of shiny brightness against the dull-colored carpet. My pulse quickened. Tears of relief and joy stung my eyes as I bent down to pick it up.

I snatched up the coin, clasping it tightly in my palm, tears streaming down my cheeks. *I am where I am supposed to be. I am doing what I am supposed to do.*

Only later, inside my vehicle, did I think to look at the date: 2005.

Jacob was born in 2005.

Still Searching

Journal entry on July 6, 2013

In the quiet morning hours I search for answers; in devotionals, the Bible, and in books by authors I respect. This morning it is Anne Lamott's *Help, Thanks, Wow* and these words that touch my heart:

> Help. Help us walk through this. Help us come through. . . .
>
> There are no words for the broken hearts of people losing people so I ask God, with me in tow, to respond to them with graciousness and encouragement enough for the day. Everyone we love and for whom we pray with such passion will die, which is the one real fly in the ointment. So we pray for miracles—please help this friend live, please help that friend die gracefully—and we pray for the survivors to somehow come through. (page 16)

A few days ago it was *The One Year Book of Hope* by Nancy Guthrie, who had lost two children of her own. It helps when the words are written by someone who intimately knows loss. That morning I impulsively tore out one of the pages to give to Elizabeth. Commonsense would dictate that I lay the page down on my printer and make a copy, but no, I felt such an immediate need to get the words to Elizabeth that urgency precluded any rationality. At first I felt guilty I'd defaced a book, but then I was glad for my impulse: it turned out that it was the verse on the other side of the page that Elizabeth needed to read that day.

I spend a good hour reading each morning, and then I pray, sometimes literally dropping down to my knees and crying out in anguish. "Why? Why a little boy?"

C. S. Lewis wrote, "God whispers in our pleasures, speaks in our conscience, but shouts in our pains: It is His megaphone to rouse a deaf world." How true that is.

Then I write. By working my way back through that first year of widowhood, I can clearly see how God walked with me down the path of loss. That gives me hope for the path my daughter and son-in-law must soon travel.

Tonight I attend my thirty-fifth high school reunion with some trepidation. I have not seen most of these former classmates for thirty-some years. I am not the same young girl they knew in high school. What they cannot know, what I am just realizing myself, is that I am not even the same person I was two years ago.

A Cursory Anniversary

And did you get what you wanted from this life, even so?
I did.
And what did you want?
To call myself beloved, to feel myself beloved on the earth.
                    —from Raymond Carver's poem "Late Fragment"

I'd intended to chronicle the entire day on my blog. In fact, I'd planned a lengthy and dramatic posting to go along with the milestone date: Wednesday, March 27, the first anniversary of my husband's death. It was even written in big, bold black letters on the wall calendar: ONE YEAR. As if I'd forget. I'd hoped for, perhaps even anticipated, some momentous event to report on that day. At the very least, I thought the light below the kitchen cabinet that had been on every day for a year might go out.

I'd once said to David, "If you die before me and want to send me a sign from heaven, make it blue so I'll recognize it is from you." Twice since his death a beautiful dark-winged butterfly with blue markings had appeared: the day I signed a contract for the coupon book that had been David's idea and a dreary October day when I'd washed his winter coat. A butterfly dropped from the sleeve when I took it off the clothesline. I wanted some sort of fanfare to mark this important date: a lightning bolt in the sky, a flock of black and blue butterflies appearing in the side yard, something.

It didn't exactly work that way. I certainly thought about David all day on March 27, but then I usually did anyway. I indulged in a morning pedicure, complete with a butterfly on my big toe, followed by lunch with the sisters who had helped get me through those early days after David's death. I was especially grateful that my very pregnant daughter Elizabeth joined us for the luncheon despite her due date the next day. The luncheon was the single family get-together Elizabeth had attended since Jacob's diagnosis. Childhood cancer thrusts the parents into a foreign land where very few people can understand their new world—a world that is lonely indeed. Elizabeth had discovered she was pregnant during a period when we were hopeful that a stem cell transplant would eradicate Jacob's cancer forever. We took the due date as a hopeful sign: Elizabeth's March 28 due date was also her dad's birthday.

I also enjoyed three deliveries of flowers to the house, beautiful bouquets from Elizabeth and my nieces Christina and Michelle, along with several cards arriving in the mail.

Everything—the pedicure, the flowers, cards, and the luncheon—paled against the presence of a little boy building an amazing city of blocks in my living room. Jacob smiled as I took a picture of him. I missed David all the more as I studied the beautiful brown eyes in the photo.

I don't want to face this alone, was my panicked thought. I'd never imagined being a single parent, or facing impending grandparenthood without my partner. I certainly never imagined facing the loss of a grandchild all alone. At the same time, I was glad for David's absence, for it spared him the news of Jacob's grim prognosis. I reflected back to the Sunday after David came home from the hospital after heart surgery, and another visit from Jacob.

Uncharacteristically, Jacob had come to the door all by himself. From his recliner, David spotted the thin arm of his grandson knocking. While I was prepared to discourage small visitors from tiring David out, he insisted I allow Jacob inside. Jacob entered shyly. He just stood there staring at David, arms akimbo, his little bald head covered by an Army hat. Thinking he might be fearful, I tried to break the ice by mentioning that he and his grandpa had both been in the hospital at the same time.

I may as well have been talking to the wall. Neither one of them paid any attention to me. They only had eyes for each other. At the time I'd thought how odd that was. It was as if my grandson and husband were all alone in the room and some unspoken message was being transferred between them through those matching brown eyes.

Neither looked away from the other, holding a gaze longer than was socially acceptable, and definitely not usual for them. Even as Jacob moved to the couch, his eyes never left David's face. I often wondered after David's death: *Had they known something then? Did their very souls recognize each other?* Did Jacob, closer to God than anyone else I knew, somehow sense this was the last time he would see his grandpa? Had there been a message to the little boy in David's long-held gaze? Did these two people—the six-year-old boy and the sixty-year-old man— realize something the rest of us didn't? After Jacob's terminal diagnosis, I frequently pondered that last encounter between the two of them. My renewed faith centered on a firm belief that David would be waiting for Jacob, to welcome him Home with outstretched arms. My prayer life reflected a little less certainty, consisting mostly of frantic pleas: *Please perform a miracle. If he must leave us, please let him go peacefully. Help my daughter and son-in-law get through this. Please help me help them.* I struggled to find something to be thankful for. *Thank you for the time we have had with Jacob. Thank you for a hospice nurse who understands what it is to lose a child.* The prayer I balked at for a long time? *Thy will be done, Lord. Thy will be done.*

There was a period after David's death that my oldest son, Dan, seemed full of anger. One day he'd mocked my mention of praying for Jacob.

"Prayer doesn't do anything," he'd retorted. It cut me to the core, yet I understood where he was coming from. Dan had gotten very close to his dad during his cancer. He'd prayed for him during his treatment, prayed as he watched his dad's health deteriorate after that punishing treatment, and then prayed again after David's heart attack. Still, his dad had died.

"You were there when I visited your dad that first night after his surgery. Do you remember what happened?" Dan shrugged his shoulders noncommittally. He wouldn't meet my eyes. He hadn't meant to hurt me with his comment, but he could certainly hear pain in my voice.

"Do you remember me leaning over and trying to kiss your dad's face?" Dan looked up from the ground, not comprehending my point. "I couldn't reach his face over the railing of the bed so I ended up kissing his arm and bringing his hand to my lips," I reminded him. "When I told him I loved him do you remember what he said?"

Dan tilted his head slightly, reflecting back on that day. I didn't wait for his answer.

"He said, 'Thank you.' *Thank you.* As if my love was a gift to him, when all along, he was the gift to me. *That* was an answer to a prayer. Having that kind of relationship was an answer to a prayer both your dad and I had prayed for years: that our marriage would improve. When your dad said that simple thank you, he showed me how grateful and sure he was of my love, a love that had grown and blossomed during his cancer treatment. The cancer was an unexpected answer to a prayer, and the relationship we savored for more than five years afterwards was a gift I will cherish forever. Dad died knowing he was truly loved."

Dan turned away, but not before I spotted tears in his eyes. He didn't respond, but just a month or two later it was Dan who asked if I'd prayed when I expressed anxiety over Jacob's situation.

The Force Be With You

Death is a natural part of life. Rejoice for those around you who transform into the Force.

—Yoda, The Revenge of the Sith

No one told Jacob he was dying. As long as he wasn't aware of that fact, Elizabeth and I couldn't tell Abby, Becca, or Joe, lest they accidentally say something around Jacob. Whenever Elizabeth questioned the advisability of informing Jacob, the hospice nurse reminded her he only needed to know if he wanted to know. The few times Elizabeth tentatively broached the subject, she saw a flash of fear in Jacob's eyes. She couldn't bear that, so she went out of her way to keep him as happy and carefree as any other little boy.

And he was, for as long as his health allowed. Jacob lived each day with an enthusiasm and a zest for life that inspired everyone around him. During his many hospital stays, Jacob had always saved his small prizes for his siblings at home. When he and the volunteer child life workers made cupcakes, he'd also save those for his brother and sister. And even during the short period when he was cancer free during those past two and a half years, he did not forget others: he collected toys to take to the hospital for other children going through treatment. How could we bear to lose such a generous child?

Elizabeth went into labor on the first day of April. I got the phone call around five in the morning.

"Mom's having the baby. Can you come down and stay with me?"

Becca's voice shook, with fear or excitement, I wasn't sure which. I assured her I would be right there. It was only after I hung up the phone that I wondered why she had been the one to call. When I arrived at her house a few minutes later I discovered the answer: Elizabeth and Ben weren't there.

"Why did you call? Where are your mom and dad?" I asked.

"Mom went in the ambulance and Dad followed," she said matter-of-factly. My blood ran cold with this announcement. Ambulance? Apparently Becca didn't realize this wasn't the usual scenario for giving birth. I tried to remain calm as I peppered her with questions, but my heart raced. All she knew was that she'd woken up with the commotion and had seen her mother taken away in an ambulance. Before he followed, her dad told her to call Grandma.

"She left blood in the bathtub," Becca offered helpfully.

When I called the hospital, they could tell me little more than the fact that a pregnant woman had indeed arrived by ambulance. I called Emily's cell phone and asked her to come and stay with the kids while I went to the hospital. She arrived within minutes. By this time Becca was nervously biting her lip. Emily and I kept glancing at each other as we attempted to assure Becca that everything was fine. Even to me the reassurance rang hollow.

I frantically prayed as I blindly rushed to the hospital and through the same doors of the building where David had been pronounced dead a year before. I was relieved when the person at the desk referred me to the maternity ward. Surely they wouldn't have Elizabeth in the maternity ward if anything had happened to her or the baby.

"Jacob has an appointment in Iowa City this morning," were the first words out of my daughter's mouth after the doctor assured me that both mother and baby were fine. They didn't yet know what had caused the bleeding.

"Don't worry, I'll take him. You just concentrate on having a healthy baby." I would never have admitted to anyone that I was hesitant to be alone with Jacob. His delayed speech made it difficult for me to understand him sometimes. Besides, he and Elizabeth had been a team for more than two years; she'd been with him at the hospital 24/7 and had been his main caretaker throughout the entire cancer treatment. Despite the fact that David and Jacob had shared a special bond, I was closer to Joe than I was to Jacob, a fact I regretted. While it was only natural since I'd taken care of Joe many times in the previous two years, I knew I was missing out on a relationship with a special little boy. For that reason alone, I was looking forward to spending some time with Jacob, but still nervous. What if I couldn't understand what he was saying?

I needn't have worried. Jacob didn't say much at all on the way to Iowa City, or in the hallways as we waited for his appointments. He'd brought a Gameboy Advance along with a Star Wars game that kept him entertained for most of the morning. When his blood was drawn, I knew to ask if he wanted me to cover his eyes like his mom always did, and he nodded his head. I was in awe of his bravery as he hardly flinched when the needle went in. I was grateful for the careful words of the doctor and nurses in Jacob's presence, but keenly aware that I couldn't ask any of the questions bouncing around inside my head. I wasn't sure though that any of us really wanted to know the answers to those questions.

When I asked Jacob if he'd like to have lunch in the cafeteria, his eyes lit up.

"I like mashed potatoes," I commented as I put a plate of the comfort food on my tray.

"Me too," he replied while he added a bowl to his own tray, along with French fries, a hamburger, a cup of fresh fruit, a roll, vegetables, and a slice of pie. I wasn't about to say no to any of his choices. He giggled when I told him I'd have to carry his tray because it was so heavy.

"What do you want to drink?"

"Pop!" The eagerness of the reply pained me. To be excited about such a small thing! If only a choice of drink was his biggest dilemma.

I studied Jacob's face as he eagerly ate, and the realization of what was ahead of him was too much for me. I blinked back tears.

"Why you cry, Grandma?"

"I miss Grandpa."

Jacob nodded his head. He could understand that concept, and I certainly wasn't going to tell him the truth; that I was crying about him.

I will always be grateful to baby Amy for choosing to be born on a day Jacob was scheduled to see the doctor. As a result, I was given the gift of a day spent alone with Jacob, hours of companionable silence that gave me an increased confidence to consider spending additional time alone with him. In the ensuing months, Jacob would spend several afternoons at my house setting up block cities and drawing pictures of Star Wars characters. Jacob loved anything related to Star Wars.

It was his love of Star Wars and my increased confidence interacting with Jacob that prompted me to consider taking him to the CORE Comic bookstore in Cedar Falls for "Free Comic Book Day" in May. I chose that store because my nephew Steve, an artist, would be there signing Garbage Pail Kid cards. The CORE was also offering the chance for a prize of a free autographed photo of Jeremy Bulloch, who had played Boba Fett in the Star War movies. Abby accompanied us, doting on Jacob the entire day, which he loved. Normally Abby would spend time with his sister, ignoring him.

When we arrived at the CORE, we had to stand in line to wait to get inside. The small store could only accommodate a certain number of shoppers at a time. When we reached the head of the line, I noticed the man guarding the door glancing at Jacob's bald head.

"We have a big Star Wars fan here," I introduced Jacob.

"Did you know Jeremy Bulloch, the actor who played Boba Fett, will be here in June?" the man asked. I informed him that not only were we aware of it, we were hoping to win one of the tickets for a signed photograph.

The man's eyes never left Jacob's head.

"You should talk to my boss," he said, but I wasn't paying much attention. The store had cleared out and it was our turn to enter.

"He's the one in the red shirt and the mullet over there," he persisted, but Jacob had already left my side and entered the store, so I just nodded and pushed past the man to follow.

Inside, Jacob stood staring, wide-eyed, at several displays of Star Wars merchandise. I took hold of Abby's and Jacob's hands, leading them to the table where they could choose a free comic book. Although they were informed they could have four, Jacob chose only a single issue: the Star Wars comic. Then he gravitated toward an enclosed glass case, leaning his forehead against it as he peered intently inside. When I joined him, I saw what had captured his attention: the entire case was full of Star Wars figures. I was surprised, and impressed, when my normally reticent grandson began pointing at figures, rattling off all the character's names.

Sensing someone watching us, I turned to see a long-haired man wearing a red shirt approaching.

"I hear we have a Star Wars fan in our store," he said, and Jacob nodded.

The man got down on one knee in front of Jacob, looking into his eyes before meeting mine with a questioning gaze.

"Did you know Jeremy Bulloch is going to be here next month?"

"Yeah," Jacob said, and his eyes lit up with excitement.

"We are hoping to win the autographed picture," I informed the stranger, and he looked from me to Jacob as if carefully considering his next words.

"I would like to personally invite you to meet with Mr. Bulloch alone, before the public does. And have dinner with him." I didn't know whose eyes were wider, Jacob's or mine. "Mom, too, of course," he hastened to add.

"Grandma," I corrected. "And his dad? He loves Star Wars too."

"Grandma and Dad," he agreed. "We'll work out the details later." He handed me his card, and I fumbled for one of mine in my purse.

The whole encounter was surreal. No one had mentioned cancer. I hadn't requested special treatment for Jacob. Yet he'd just nabbed a private meeting with an actor from his favorite movie. I would later ask Mike, the comic book store owner, what had prompted him to invite Jacob to the supper and a private meeting with Mr. Bulloch.

"It was Jeremy at the door. He recognized something in Jacob. Jeremy is a cancer survivor."

There was never any question I would be going with Jacob and Ben to meet the Star Wars actor, but I knew very little about the movie series. I told Jacob to choose one of his favorite movies so we could watch it together before we met Mr. Bulloch.

"Make sure it has Boba Fett in it," I said, and he giggled because I'd mispronounced the name.

"And baby Ewoks," Jacob added.

"And baby Ewoks," I agreed.

So it was that Jacob visited our home in early June for a movie date with Grandma. Jacob eagerly pointed out the baby Ewoks and the demise of Boba Fett in the film. When one of the Ewoks died, Jacob hastened to assure me that it didn't really die and would return in a later movie. I squeezed his hand at that pronouncement, not sure if that was true but acutely aware that the idea of an Ewok's death had upset Jacob. He'd allowed me to cuddle against him a little when he thought I was scared by the plot. My girls laughed at how seriously I seemed to be taking the movie. I promised Jacob I would watch another episode with him someday, but viewing just that one film at least helped me become familiar with the characters Jacob continually mentioned. For as little as Jacob talked, when it came to Star Wars, he practically jabbered.

I will treasure forever the memory of that day spent with Ben, Jacob, the actor, and a group of men dressed in full Star Wars regalia. Especially the look in Jacob's eyes as the dignified English gentleman spent an hour catering to the whims of a small child. Jeremy Bulloch's intriguing British accent seemed to relax Jacob, although he never spoke a word outside of his repeated "yeah."

When Mr. Bulloch told Jacob he could pick out anything in the store, his eyes sparkled with delight when Jacob chose a replica Boba Fett helmet, which the star immediately autographed with a flourish. A team of Mandalorian Mercs, a Star Wars costume club, had also heard about the terminally ill child. They brought him a helmet they'd designed, presenting it to him and dubbing him a lifetime honorary member of their organization. As Ben and I watched from the sidelines, television and newspaper reporters' cameras flashed. For one amazing day, Jacob was the star whose smile lit up a room.

That evening I sat across from Jeremy Bulloch and Jacob at the dinner table. I watched as Jeremy, who seemed to speak Jacob's silent language fluently, drummed his fingers up and down on the edge of the table, as if playing a piano. A delighted Jacob mimicked the actor's actions. My throat filled with tears. I met Ben's eyes across the table, where he sat straight with pride next to his son. He was enjoying the show just as much as I was. Jacob was in his element, interacting with an actor from his favorite movie. The other men at the table were part of the set: Mike, the owner of the comic book store, who had made the entire thing possible, and the Mandalorin Mercs, new friends of the little boy who had become one of their own, a comrade in distress.

Lights Out

To live is to suffer; to survive is to find meaning in the suffering.
—Viktor Frankl, Holocaust survivor

The kitchen light I had left on twenty-four hours a day for more than 450 days since my husband's death, began flickering and wildly flashing on June 24, Jacob's eighth birthday.

"The kitchen light is going out," my son Dan announced ominously in the doorway. I got up from my desk chair and joined him in the kitchen. We just stood there for a moment in silence, considering the timing. *Why this particular day after more than 450 days of burning brightly for twenty-four hours a day?*

"Stop it. I know what you're thinking, and it doesn't mean that Jacob's light is fading, or anything like that." Dan warned as we stared at the flashing that seemed to have a particular pattern. Dan snorted in derision when I asked if he knew Morse code.

The light went out, and that was, indeed, Jacob's last day of feeling healthy. Jacob had begun experiencing some pain in his chest and side, which we'd hoped was from playing a fierce game of Wii tennis with his aunt Rachel the weekend before. However, the pain quickly progressed to difficulty in breathing. The doctor prescribed morphine and oxygen for Jacob, advising against draining the fluid that was building up in his chest since it would inevitably return, probably within a week.

The tumor that had gone from his kidney to his lung was growing rapidly, despite that last-ditch clinical trial drug study and additional radiation treatment. In early July the hospice nurse informed us it was just a matter of days. By then Jacob was on oxygen and morphine twenty-four hours a day.

For several mornings I'd rise at 3:00 a.m., get in the car in my pajamas, and drive past Elizabeth and Ben's house, searching for lights or some sign of activity. Would tonight be the night? Did Elizabeth need me? I'd answer the phone every morning with trepidation: *Was this the day?* After a couple of weeks of this, I had to stop. I couldn't continue to anticipate Jacob's death that way. It was becoming obvious that it was not going to be the few days the nurse had predicted.

A few days turned into a mind-boggling fifty-one. For *fifty-one* days my daughter cared for Jacob as he lay on the couch dying. She slept on a mattress on the floor so as to be near him as he grew weaker and weaker. One morning, as she rose uncomfortably to a sitting position, she cried out with the stiffness, complaining of a sore back. A thin arm reached out from beneath the blankets on the couch and a small hand began rubbing her back. Jacob had heard her comment and was attempting to rub the stiffness and pain away from his beloved mother.

I held back from seeing Jacob much during those weeks. He wanted only his mother, and I wasn't sure I could handle seeing him like that. I stopped by to pick up his siblings and take them away, but I rarely went inside the house. After several days of this, I knew I must face the sight that my daughter faced daily. Inside, I approached the couch tentatively. Would I upset him? A few times when I had visited, he'd hidden his face in a blanket. I reached out hesitantly, touching his thin arm, the skin hot and dry as paper. He didn't move, but I could see the rise and fall of his swollen chest. Suddenly, my legs gave way, and I dropped to my knees in front of the grandson that I loved so dearly. My hand shook as I lifted it to his soft, fuzzy head. I felt as though I was in the presence of someone very holy.

"I love you," I whispered, and when he didn't respond, an even softer whisper, "Tell Grandpa that I love him and miss him." And then, with a groan, "*Dear God, don't let him suffer.*"

Edna, the Hospice nurse, couldn't explain why Jacob was holding on so long, as this sort of tumor typically stopped a heart beating long before this. She'd stopped taking his vitals because he didn't want her to touch him. She insisted that Jacob be allowed to control whatever he could. One day toward the end, my daughter asked her to check Jacob because he hadn't been responding that day. As Edna moved her stethoscope around his chest, her eyes widened.

"I've never seen this happen before," she whispered. "No wonder his heart hasn't stopped. It has moved over to the other side of his chest."

Jacob endured one very bad day on August 18, constantly calling out and moving restlessly. No amount of medication seemed to calm him down until late in the day. I took the other children away so they wouldn't see their brother that way, but my mother's heart remained there with my daughter and son-in-law. That evening, my daughter sat on the couch next to her sleeping son and told him that it was okay to go, that she would soon join him.

Jacob died sometime during that night as his mother slept.

I felt numb for several days after Jacob's death. I wondered where God was on Sunday when Jacob was crying out in pain. I did not feel Him when my daughter called the next morning to tell me Jacob had died sometime during the night. Instead, all I felt was an uncomfortable sort of relief: Jacob was no longer suffering. The long ordeal of caregiving had ended for my daughter. I looked for a sign—*anything* that would tell me God was there in all of *this*. I did not pick up a pen and write words of thanksgiving as I had the morning after my husband's death.

My heart felt like lead in my chest all day Monday and most of Tuesday. I went with my daughter and son-in-law to the funeral home to make plans for a wake, and then to the church to plan a funeral. All the while, I was reminded of the plans so recently made for the husband I had lost. *My beloved, my beloved, I need you!* I did not know if it was my husband or God I called out for. I wanted some sign that God was with me. That David was nearby. Instead, I just felt empty. Spent. How much grief can one heart bear? In the space of three years I had lost my mother, my husband, and now my grandson.

Where are you God? I wondered as reality set in and I knew I would never again look into Jacob's beautiful brown eyes, never hear his delighted giggle, at least not on this earth.

The morning before Jacob's wake, a woman messaged me on Facebook, telling me about some magazines she'd picked up at the library: "Yesterday I picked up some used magazines at the library to read. . . . This morning I was putting a couple of them in my bag . . . and a slip of paper fell out; . . . it was a receipt from the library with the due date on it. . . . The name was David Kenyon . . . so I said a prayer for you on the way to work. . . . Ironic how God uses a small piece of paper to bring you to the mind of others."

I initially shrugged at the coincidence, until it dawned on me how rarely David had used his own library card to check anything out and obviously hadn't checked anything out for over seventeen months. I thought then to ask the title of the magazine: *Wild Bird*, said her return e-mail. I felt a small prickle at the back of my neck.

Wild Bird. Before his death, David had been telling me I was "flying, soaring." Jacob had earned his own wings.

Despite this obvious message, I still felt angry. For the first time since David's death, I was feeling a clear, unmistakable anger. That evening I went to bed furious with God. *How could he have allowed this?*

I had a dream that night:

A healthy Jacob was climbing up into my lap. He was tall, with a full head of hair. I could feel the heaviness of his body. He turned in my lap and I felt the insistent push of feet and legs against one of my arms as he attempted to be cradled sideways, like an infant. In my dream, I looked to my daughter Elizabeth to see if it was all right that I cradle her son, this big boy, like a baby, and she nodded.

"I could literally feel the heaviness of holding Jacob in my arms as I woke up," I told Elizabeth on the phone the next morning. Both of us took comfort in the vividness of the dream.

Is there meaning in the death of an innocent child? The morning my daughter announced Jacob's death on the "Jacob's Ladder" Facebook page we'd begun when he was diagnosed, seventeen thousand people viewed the status. By evening, I saw the number of viewers was over fifty-six thousand. By the next morning, that number exceeded sixty-four thousand. *Sixty-four thousand* people on Facebook heard about a small boy from Iowa who had touched the lives of so many people. *Sixty-four thousand people!* We could live to be eighty years old and not touch even a fraction of that population.

My daughter and I were determined to make Jacob's life and death meaningful. Because of Jacob, we wanted to become better people. "You can become bitter or better," I'd heard said, and we all knew someone who'd become bitter with grief. We didn't want to become those people. In Jacob's honor, and through his example, we decided we would strive to live a life filled with kindness. Just as Jacob had done on his deathbed, reaching out to his mother, we would reach out to others. We designed "random acts of kindness" cards that related our loss and the reason for the kind act, listing the web address of the "Jacob's Ladder" Facebook page. Then we began doing random acts of kindness and asking others to do the same. We mailed out cards, and many who followed his page designed their own. Friends, family, and total strangers began doing random acts of kindness all over the United States in Jacob's memory, and soon we were seeing stories posted on the "Jacob's Ladder" page. The life of one small boy had made a difference in the world, and would continue to do so. We felt blessed to be a part of that difference.

Grief at Seventeen and a Half Months

Blog post on September 8, 2013

What does grief look like at ten and a half weeks, twenty weeks, or one year? The woman or man who has recently lost their spouse might wonder that. I know I did, and I looked for answers in books written by those who had gone down the grieving road before me. Madeleine L'Engle, C. S. Lewis, H. Norman Wright, Joan Didion, and Joyce Carol Oates were a few of the many authors I looked to for guidance and insight. While I knew my own journey might not mirror theirs, it gave me an idea of what I might expect as I navigated the darkness of spousal loss.

My hope is that someone who picks up my future book ten weeks after their own loss will immediately recognize the frantic, crazed thoughts in the first journal entry as their own. If not, then hurray for them—they might not need my book, but they may want to continue to read it anyway, just to see how that frantic, crazed woman fared.

When a grieving person hears the well-intentioned, "You look like you are doing well," they might hear (as I often did), an underlying message: *You must not have loved him/her enough to have red-rimmed eyes and tear-stained cheeks at all times; to have already removed the ring, to laugh, to have gone back to work. You have not remained prostrate on the ground, tearing your clothes, gashing your arms with sharp objects and shaving your head in grief-stricken anguish?*

You who have never "been there" in the throes of grief, have **no idea** what is going on inside the head of the grieving spouse: the scattered thoughts, the constant worry that we will forget something or someone in our fog-induced state, that strange feeling of not quite "being all there" when out in social situations, the pall that covers everything, like a cloak of sadness that never lifts.

I *am* doing well, most days. My journal entries inform me of that fact. I didn't journal nearly as often one year after David's death as I had in those first months. By sharing a few private entries in my book, my hope is that the reader will also see the positive progression. Mine will be a book of hope and growth after loss.

So, what does grief look like (for me) after seventeen and a half months? From my journal a couple of days ago:

Sept. 3, 2013

Today I pulled all of the weeds out of the raised bed in the back yard. While that might seem a small feat to most people, to me it was huge. The raised bed was David's; the gardening, his chore. Just as I couldn't turn off the kitchen light that he'd always turned off and on, I've refused to touch the tools in the garage or weed the raised bed. It seems ridiculous, I know. It felt good to rip out the tall grass and weeds, even as rivulets of sweat ran down my face in the hot sun. I felt something small flicker inside me, and then grow. It was as though working hard in the backyard, tearing out weeds and sweating profusely brought a distinct shift in my attitude. It was as if I'd turned a corner in my grieving. It dawned on me then—I feel alive! Have I just been "going through the motions" these past seventeen months?

The next day I tackled the back porch, carting pop cans to the local Walmart, flattening empty cardboard boxes, tasks David had normally done. I sorted through the mess that had built up since last year so we could comfortably walk through the porch again. The day after that, I stained the deck using a can of stain David had purchased just a month before he died. He'd swiped just one small corner of the deck to make sure he liked the Redwood color, and then he'd stained the picnic table. He hadn't gotten to the deck before his death. It felt good to accomplish something so simple, something David had intended doing, as if I was completing the task in his honor. By this time, my girls were asking me what was going on and why I was doing so much. My heart sank as I realized just how little I *had* been doing around the house.

Next, it was time to tackle my bedroom. I approached the task with two trash bags and one large box: one bag for donation items, and one for actual garbage. The box was for whatever I decided to store on a high shelf of the closet. I cleaned off the top of the dresser first, smelling each bottle of cologne and settling on just three bottles to keep. The box of matches brought a particular pain: *my romantic husband liked candle-light.* I'd thrown the cinnamon candle away immediately after his death, but the matches had remained there for seventeen months. The matches were set aside for a downstairs cupboard drawer, the cologne was added to the storage box along with some odd spare keys I didn't know what else to do with. The top drawer of the dresser was next: David's billfold, two black combs, his T-shirts, and one pair of pajama pants went into the box, creating an empty dresser drawer for me. *This isn't so bad,* I thought. In fact, it was easy! With renewed strength, I approached the closet, shaking my head at how long it had taken me to deal with David's shirts. One by one, I removed the favorites I had left hanging in the closet, carefully folding them and adding them to the box. One well-worn belt was added, two others discarded. It was then that I noticed a small pile of clothing in the corner of the closet: the heavier sweat-shirts David wore in the winter. Before carefully folding his favorite Iowa Hawkeye shirt, I looked toward the open bedroom door. Realizing no one was near, I brought the shirt close to my nose. *How can this be?* I wondered as I recognized the familiar scent. I buried my face in it, sniff-ing deeply.

This is what grief looks like at seventeen and a half months, I decided. *A woman who manages to accomplish some long-overdue household chores her husband had always taken care of. A woman who disposes of her husband's belts and cologne.*

A woman sobbing into her deceased husband's sweatshirt.

A Room of One's Own

A woman must have money and a room of her own if she is to write fiction.

—Virginia Woolf

For the first three nights after David's death, only Matthew slept upstairs. The rest of us slept fitfully downstairs, strewn across couch cushions and the floor like dirty laundry. I knew I eventually had to face going back upstairs, so the night of David's funeral the girls and I each chose one of David's t-shirts to sleep with and I slept on a mattress on the floor of Katie and Abby's room. I continued doing so for several days. When I eventually braved my own bed, Abby followed me, and the truth was that I welcomed her familiar presence. I wasn't sure at first that I wanted to be alone.

When Matthew moved out in August and Katie moved into his empty room, it seemed a perfect time to transition Abby back to her own bed. I tried to wean her off my presence by sleeping on a mattress on the floor next to her bed, but she tossed and turned for two hours before we gave up on that idea. We repeated the same scenario night after night, with no success, until one night she began crying and I responded in fury at the ridiculousness of the situation. I was immediately ashamed. I was yelling at a fatherless child! I knew without a doubt that David would be horrified that I'd gotten so upset over something so inconsequential. I stopped pressuring her to leave my room and agreed to wait until July, and Abby's tenth birthday, to try again. It would be fifteen months after

131

her dad's death. The plan was that on her tenth birthday, Abby would return to her own bed in her own bedroom. As an incentive, I'd promised that Becca could spend the night.

Abby and Becca played late into the night on Abby's birthday. As I followed the two into Abby's room to tuck them in, my heart sank. I could tell by the set of her shoulders that Abby was not going to accomplish her goal of sleeping in her own room, even with Becca. Two hours later, I still heard frantic whispers from the next room. Knowing I wasn't going to get any sleep until they did, I hissed at the two girls from my room, "Just get in here and take my bed."

Chastened, both Becca and Abby fell asleep easily in the big bed David and I had shared at one time. As I fell asleep an idea came to me.

I asked Abby the next morning "Why are you able to fall asleep easily in my room and seem unable to sleep in your own room, even with me? Is it the bed, or the room?"

Abby seemed to ponder the question for a moment.

"I think it is both."

She was surprised, but agreeable, when I suggested then that we trade rooms. The mattress I'd shared with my husband was more to his liking than mine anyway. I actually preferred Abby's new memory foam mattress.

The musical-bed arrangement wasn't exactly a new development after David's death. It had begun the November before. In early November 2011, I'd attended a writer's conference in Kansas and was gone for several days. When I returned, I discovered that Abby had taken my space in our bed.

"I slept with Dad while you were gone so he wouldn't be lonely," she'd informed me, and David shook his head imperceptibly when he noted I was going to make an issue of it. She'd slept in her own bed for weeks afterwards with no problem, until one night shortly before Christmas when she came to our bed. David and I thought perhaps she was having bad dreams and rather than fight it, we assumed it was something temporary. She'd usually go to David's side of the bed, but if I saw her standing there before he did, I'd get out and motion her to come to my side. Then I'd go to her room and immediately fall asleep in her bed with no problem. David tried to do the same, moving to Abby's bed so as not to wake me, but he didn't sleep well on her firmer mattress so I ended up in her bed far more often than he did.

It was me in our bed with Abby that March 2012 night when David shook me awake because he was feeling so ill. She raised her head at our whispered exchange.

"Be quiet," she said.

I leaned over to whisper, "Daddy is feeling sick. I need to take care of him."

I was surprised when she obligingly got up and headed back to her room without further comment. David lay down and I went to the bathroom for a cold washcloth. He visibly relaxed as I wiped his clammy forehead, and then fell asleep as I held his hand.

The prospect of redesigning Abby's room as my own was exciting. Except for a couple of months in the summer of 1978 when I'd lived with my brother Lyle and his wife before beginning college, I'd never had a room of my own. For several weeks I worked at the transformation. Katie and Abby got into the spirit of things: Katie painting the walls a light blue (conducive to creativity) and both of them helping me rearrange furniture and organize. I traded dressers with Katie, a move that forced me to confront David's cologne bottles I still had on the top of mine, along with the drawer full of his t-shirts. Abby claimed a couple to sleep in, and everything else went into a single box for storage.

I ordered butterfly curtains and a butterfly bedspread online and found butterfly wall decals on clearance at a local discount store. I hung a beautiful blue butterfly painting from Emily on one wall and unearthed a painting my mother had given David and me for our twenty-fifth anniversary on another. I picked up a bamboo shelf and a rug at my sister's consignment store and she contributed a glass-topped end table. The shelf held a memorial candle with David's photo, teddy bears my mother had made me, some ceramic birds from David, and several devotional books. The top shelf held a lovely book crafted by the same young woman who'd shared notebook pages full of Bible verses with me shortly after David's death. She'd painted a vintage book bright blue, gluing some of the pages together in an arch. Then she designed butterflies that looked like they were flying up out of the pages. Dan had begun dating this young woman around the same time that he'd become more open to prayer, nearly ten months after his dad's death.

Nineteen months after my husband's death I sat in my new room, a cup of tea at my side and the soft glow of a lamp on the end table illuminating the pad of paper I write on. I reflected back on the winter after my mother's death and the hours spent in her empty house, encouraged by my supportive husband to take time for my writing. During those weeks sitting at her table, I got more writing done than I had in the previous two years combined.

My thoughts turned to that March 2012 morning as I sat across from my husband at the kitchen table and he marveled at how far I'd come in my writing and workshops.

"You're flying! You're soaring," he'd said, and I reminded him it was because of him I could do those things. As I gazed at the butterflies on the walls of my room, the curtains and the bedspread, I thought about the man who had become "the wind beneath my wings."

The room of my own became an oasis of sorts, a quiet place where I could write, read, pray, and, occasionally, sleep.

A Force Stronger Than Death
Blog post on September 15, 2013

Seven women are in a van headed home after a "Girls Night Out" at a Michael Bublé concert and an overnight stay in Omaha, Nebraska. There is nothing remarkable about that, except perhaps for the woman in the passenger side of the front seat. "Go to a concert" had been on her and her husband's "bucket list."

Her husband had died before that wish had been fulfilled. Before "travel together," "ride an airplane," or many other goals had been fulfilled. "When our children are grown up," had become "Never." At least, never together.

There is an incessant pall over everything after a loss of a spouse, even at a Michael Bublé concert that had the woman shivering with excitement as she waited in line with the group of new friends. The friends and the concert were courtesy of her longtime, good friend Mary.

The woman did not fail to notice the couple seated directly in front of her nuzzling each other's necks, the man whispering sweet nothings into his wife's ear just like her own husband had. When she saw the man put his hand into the back pocket of the woman's jeans she had to look away, dizzy with longing. Her husband had always done that.

The concert begins and the grieving woman begins to sway a little with the music, reveling in an unaccustomed joy.

"We have a special guest in the audience," Michael Bublé announces, and images of running football players flash on a screen above. *Is there a famous football player in the audience?* the woman wonders, just before she spots a small boy running with the team. She experiences a sinking sensation as the cameras pan to the small bald boy in the front row. "Oh, Mary, I'm so sorry," her friend comments as the room starts to spin. Her friend's hug steadies her as tears stream down her cheeks, unchecked. She sobs. Because nearly seventeen months after her beloved died, less than a month before this concert, the woman had also lost her eight-year-old grandson to cancer.

The heavy pall of sadness does lift sometime during the concert, and the remainder of the night is sweet with beautiful music and lovely new friends. The next morning brings coffee and continued conversation; getting to know a group of women hand-picked by her friend. Of course she would love them; they all love her dear friend Mary!

Which brings us back to the van and the trip home. After a stop for gas, a surprised comment comes from Chris, one of the women who had been in the same seat on the way to Nebraska: "Look what I just found. What is this? Does Frankie still play video games?"

There is laughter; the son in question is in college.

"What is it?" Evelyn, the driver and owner of the vehicle asks, turning a little in her seat.

"A Gameboy Advance game."

As the game is passed to the front, the bereaved grandmother sitting in the passenger seat feels a distinct prickle at the back of her neck. Her grandson Jacob loved playing Gameboy games. He'd entertained himself with them through dozens of procedures and doctor's appointments during his two-and-a-half-year battle with cancer.

She holds out her hand and someone places the game in her palm. Even before she turns it over, she knows. Jacob loved Star Wars. He was obsessed with the movies, the characters, and the games.

It is a Star Wars game. The woman just sits there, not moving, stunned into silence. She can barely talk around the lump forming in her throat.

"Did your son own a Gameboy Advance?" she finally asks. Evelyn just shrugs her shoulders.

"Even if he ever did, I've cleaned out the van several times since he would have played a game."

The woman is quiet for several miles, closing her eyes and pretending to be asleep. There is background conversation going on around her, but her thoughts are far beyond the confines of the vehicle.

During the remainder of the trip, the woman wonders just how to approach Evelyn about the game. It seems a silly thing to ask for, and yet she can't get it out of her mind. When Evelyn parks her van, she gets up her courage to stammer, "Can I have this game?" Evelyn shrugs her shoulders again, "Sure."

The woman clutches the talisman all the way home, as if holding it could give her strength. She misses her husband. She misses her grandson.

Once home, she tells her daughters about the game. Her seventeen-year-old daughter asks for it, and then pops it into her sister's Gameboy.

"This is cool. There is a game saved on here." The room is silent while she pushes a button to start the saved game.

"There is a back story that just popped up," the daughter says, beginning to read in her head. She looks up and her widened eyes meet her mother's expectant ones. Then she reads out loud:

"The Force is stronger than death."

Epilogue:
December 2013

The holes in your heart never fill in. They simply quit bleeding so pro-fusely.
—Judith Robl, writer and personal friend who suffered her own loss of three grandchildren

Had the loss of my mother, and then David, prepared me in any way for the loss of Jacob? Loss piled upon loss, piled upon loss, but with the loss of Jacob, there was that additional grief of knowing there was nothing I could do, nothing I could say, to make the pain go away for my daughter and son-in-law.

"Loss is loss," I'd heard said at a grief support group, but I'm not so sure. The loss of my mother could not compare to the loss of my husband. Nor had the loss of a husband prepared me for the loss of my grandson. Each loss was different and I could not know, did not want to know, what it was to lose a child.

"You won't always feel this way," I assured Elizabeth early on, careful to avoid saying "it will get better," because I knew the loss would never go away, that the hole in the hearts of Elizabeth and Ben would never be filled.

Twenty-one months after his death, David was still a huge part of my life, his insight and wisdom guiding me in my life without him, his wise words echoing in my head: *Slow down, things will get done. Don't worry so much. Just tell the truth.* I learned so much from David in the years I'd shared with him.

"I wish that David could have been married to the woman I am now," I confided to a Bible study class I led on fear and anxiety, but I'm not sure that those present understood my lament. David had kept me balanced, had always been there to calm my anxiety, had "talked me down" when I was frantic with worry. When he died, I lost that balance, and it practically unhinged me. The bleakest night of those early days sent me to a doctor's office the next morning, where I was prescribed an anti-anxiety drug my doctor had warned me wouldn't take the sadness away. But that bottle of pills sits untouched in my cupboard twenty-one months later. It turns out I discovered a substitute for medication.

"You're a different person than you were before David's death," my friend Mary observed in a recent letter. Mary, who has known me for over twenty-five years, intimately knew of my struggles with anxiety and was surprised at how nonchalantly I was taking certain things that would have previously upset me.

"The worst has happened. I lost David. Nothing else can compare, or hardly matters, in relation to that," I'd written back.

I lost the man I'd loved for nearly thirty-four years, the father of my eight children, my rock, the "wind beneath my wings." I'd finally learned what it was to truly love someone, and then, in an instant, he was gone. The love remained, however. I can honestly say I still love David, will always love David, even while my heart is open to loving someone else someday.

In the midst of the darkness of loss, I found light. Admittedly, in those first weeks, it might have been but a single small spark I sensed deep inside of me, but that spark guided me in the twisted, dark journey of grief. As I stumbled over the roots of hopelessness and despair, that light grew to illuminate my path, a path I sometimes felt very alone on. At some point in the journey I'd turned around, and there was God.

That is grace.

Who Am I . . . Two Years Out

Blog post on March 30, 2014

"I have a confession to make. I still cry about your dad. Every single morning." The stunned silence of my daughters filled the room and alarm crossed each of their faces. In just a few days it would be two years since David died and Rachel, Emily, Katie, and I were reminiscing about the particular horror of those days that followed his death.

I'd meant my comment as a good thing; that I wasn't forgetting their dad. I hastened to explain, "Not a lot. Sometimes just a few tears. When everyone else is asleep and I'm all alone downstairs, sometimes I just sit and cry for a few minutes. Other times it's just a sob or two that escapes. Then it's over, and I go about my day."

Three pairs of widened eyes stared at me in apparent horror.

"I don't think I wanted to know that," one of my daughters finally commented, and the other two nodded.

Why hadn't it occurred to me that my daughters might like to think their mother was completely and gloriously happy? Maybe because it had been obvious from our conversation that they weren't "getting over" the loss of their dad anytime soon, and I'd wanted to reassure them that that was a perfectly normal response?

What is life like two years after the loss of David? A better question might be *what am I like?*

Who are you? I'd wondered just days before when I'd asked a stranger if I could hug her. She'd stopped at my library to ask if I was the one who'd written a book on cancer. When I told her that I was, she began telling me about her husband. As soon as she said the word *cancer*, my breath caught in my throat. I recognized the waver in her voice and the tears glinting in her eyes. This was a woman in emotional turmoil.

"The doctors have told him to put his affairs in order," she continued, and I glanced down at the tote bag near my feet as my heart lurched with her words. Suddenly I understood the compulsion to add one of my books to the tote that morning, despite the fact that I'd already added it to our library shelf. . . . I had learned to listen to those "small, quiet urgings" of the heart.

"You don't happen to have one of your books with you?" she asked, and I pulled it out and handed it to her.

"You can have it." This was the third copy I'd given away in a week. It was occurring to me that perhaps this was going to be a book I would be giving away more than selling. There are a lot of hurting people in the world, a lot of cancer patients and caregivers. I immediately nudged away any lingering worries about how exactly I would pay for those books I was giving away. *People above material*, I reminded myself. It was then I asked the woman if I could give her a hug.

"I was going to ask you for one," she sheepishly admitted as I came around the desk and my arms encircled her. A single sob escaped her as I tightened the embrace. Just two years ago, I'm not sure I would have known to hug her. Before my husband's cancer in 2006, the possibility wouldn't even have crossed my mind. I rarely hugged anyone back then, outside of my own family; and even then, the hugs sometimes felt forced and awkward.

After she left, I sat at my desk and cried a little, considering the very real possibility that this woman in her forties would likely need my up-coming grief book by the end of the year.

My daughter Elizabeth snorted with apparent bemusement when I related the encounter to her on the phone that evening. "You hugged her? A complete stranger? Who are you?"

Exactly. *Who am I?* Who is this woman who lived most of the first fifty years of her life not trusting others, particularly females because they had been her biggest tormentors in elementary school? How did the woman with only a handful of friends outside of her siblings become the kind of person who would reach out to hug a stranger, and then shed tears of empathy for her?

I think of my mother, who on bus trips would come home with

names and addresses of strangers she had befriended; and my husband, who during and after his cancer treatment would casually fling his arm around someone's shoulder or tell them that he loved them. *Loved them!* I remember feeling envious of the ease in which he said those words. A mutual friend of ours in line at his wake told me how much it had meant to her that the last time she'd seen him, he'd thrown his arms around her and blurted out that he loved her. Loved *her.* . . . I'd been standing next to him that day, and I remember clearly my reaction: the initial surprise at his words, then the immediate understanding (she was sweet, caring, and seemed very alone in the world), followed by a swift and sharp envy.

"That is so nice you hugged her and told her you loved her," I'd told him in the car on the way home. "I wish I could be more like you in that way."

And now I am. I am saddened that it took the loss of a special man for me to become more like the best in him.

I am surprised that my normally reticent self has become so effusive. Losing David and Jacob has truly *refined* me. The woman I have become is a much nicer, more loving, more empathetic one than the woman I once was. It occurs to me that I am now who God meant me to be all along.

During those initial dark days after the loss of David, I felt as though I was stumbling around in darkness. *How do I do this? How will I go on? How can I stand this pain?* I didn't yet know how to search for answers to those questions in the Bible, so I grasped onto the words of others who had gone down this path before me: C. S. Lewis, Madeleine L'Engle, H. Norman Wright, Joan Didion. I read a dozen books related to grief in those first weeks, jotting down passages and pertinent words in my journal.

And I prayed. One answer to prayer came in the form of a writing assignment for an upcoming grief Bible. If I were to write devotions to be included in that Bible, then I would have to learn how to study the Bible for answers.

Those words were the seeds planted—words that sprouted and blossomed in my soul. I can see that now. Looking back on the last two years, I clearly see the instances when God reached out through others to touch my life, to help me through loss:

> The immediate "surrounding of the guard," in the form of sisters who were at my side within minutes of my returning home from the hospital where David was pronounced dead.
>
> My friend Mary Humston, who somehow knew exactly what to do and what to say to help me through.
>
> Women at the breakfast table during a writer's conference, women, who when they discovered it was my first wedding anniversary without my husband, immediately clutched each other's hands and surrounded me with prayer. A simple paper sign posted on a tree on the path back to my room, a sign that was not there just an hour before: "If a tree does not suffer great winds and storms, its bark will not grow thick and strong. The tree, thin, naked, and weak, will fall over and die. Storms will bring strength, majesty, and growth. God brings storms to build us. When he builds us, we will go forward."
>
> A young woman who knew our family, not knowing exactly why, but feeling led to, writes out Bible verses on notebook paper and drops them in the mail. "I felt called out to write some verses down for you," she had written, and the verses were exactly what I had prayed for, had actually requested from someone else, but never received. "I need Bible verses that will comfort me. Can you help me find them?" I'd asked. Within days the Holy Spirit prompted this young woman, a young woman who, two years later, is to become my daughter-in-law, to jot down verses that would help me.

This is how God has worked in the last two years, through others who have followed those inexplicable urgings of the heart and reached out to me. It is how God is now working in me.

Bring another copy of your book to work, I heard, and not two hours later a hurting woman who is caring for a husband with cancer walked into my library and asked for it.

Suggested Resources

Books

Companion Through the Darkness: Inner Dialogues on Grief, by Stephanie Ericsson

Getting to the Other Side of Grief, by Susan J. Zonnebelt-Smeenge and Robert C. De Vries

Good Grief: A Novel, by Lolly Winston (fictional account of a widow's grief)

A Grief Observed, by C. S. Lewis

Help, Thanks, Wow: The Three Essential Prayers, by Anne Lamott

The Joy Diet: 10 Daily Practices for a Happier Life, by Martha Beck

Knowing God, Knowing Myself: An Invitation to Daily Discovery, by Cecil Murphey

Making Sense When Life Doesn't: The Secrets of Thriving in Tough Times, by Cecil Murphey

NIV Hope in the Mourning Bible, edited by Timothy Beals

The One Year Book of Hope, by Nancy Guthrie

The Other Side of Sadness: What the New Science of Bereavement Tells Us About Life After Loss, George A. Bonanno

Reflections of a Grieving Spouse, by H. Norman Wright

The Truth About Grief: The Myth of Its Five Stages and the New Science of Loss, by Ruth Davis Konigsberg

Two-Part Invention: The Story of a Marriage (Crosswicks Journal, Book 4) by Madeleine L'Engle

The Year of Magical Thinking, by Joan Didion

Websites

Compassionate Friends
www.compassionatefriends.org, supports families after a child dies, 650 chapters in all fifty states

GriefNet.org
Internet community of persons dealing with grief, death, and major loss, fifty e-mail support groups, two support groups (one for adults and one for kids at KIDSAID.com), a safe environment for grieving kids and their parents

GriefShare.org
Grief recovery support group, with online, e-mail, and in-person support

Hospice Foundation of America
www.hospicefoundation.org, end-of-life resources, along with information about grief support

National Widower's Organization
www.nationalwidowers.org, support group for men who have lost a spouse

About the Author

Mary Potter Kenyon graduated from the University of Northern Iowa with a BA in Psychology and is the Director of the Winthrop Public Library. She is widely published in magazines, newspapers, and anthologies, including five Chicken Soup books. Her essay on the connection between grief and creativity was published in the January/February 2013 issue of *Poets & Writers* magazine and she has several devotions included in the *NIV Hope in the Mourning Bible* released by Zondervan in 2013. Mary writes a weekly couponing column for the Dubuque Telegraph Herald newspaper and conducts writing and couponing workshops for women's groups, libraries, and community colleges. Mary's public speaking repertoire includes the topics of couponing, writing, utilizing your talents in your everyday life, and finding hope and healing in grief. *Coupon Crazy: The Science, the Savings, and the Stories Behind America's Extreme Obsession* was published by Familius in 2013. *Chemo-Therapist: How Cancer Cured a Marriage* was released in April 2014. Mary lives in Manchester, Iowa, with three of her eight children.

About Familius

Welcome to a place where mothers are celebrated, not compared. Where heart is at the center of our families, and family at the center of our homes. Where boo boos are still kissed, cake beaters are still licked, and mistakes are still okay. Welcome to a place where books—and family—are beautiful. Familius: a book publisher dedicated to helping families be happy.

Visit Our Website: www.familius.com

Our website is a different kind of place. Get inspired, read articles, discover books, watch videos, connect with our family experts, download books and apps and audiobooks, and along the way, discover how values and happy family life go together.

Join Our Family

There are lots of ways to connect with us! Subscribe to our newsletters at www.familius.com to receive uplifting daily inspiration, essays from our Pater Familius, a free ebook every month, and the first word on special discounts and Familius news.

Become an Expert

Familius authors and other established writers interested in helping families be happy are invited to join our family and contribute online content. If you have something important to say on the family, join our expert community by applying at:

www.familius.com/apply-to-become-a-familius-expert

Get Bulk Discounts

If you feel a few friends and family might benefit from what you've read, let us know and we'll be happy to provide you with quantity discounts. Simply email us at specialorders@familius.com.

Website: www.familius.com
Facebook: www.facebook.com/paterfamilius
Twitter: @familiustalk, @paterfamilius1
Pinterest: www.pinterest.com/familius

The most important work

you ever do will be within the

walls of your own home.

CPSIA information can be obtained at www.ICGtesting.com
Printed in the USA
BVOW07s0804060914

365263BV00001B/2/P